LIP SERVICE

Also by the author

Plays

A Star Fell
Girls Will Be Girls
Invictus

White Skin, Dark Skin, Power, Dream:
Collected Essays on Literature and Culture

LIP SERVICE

A PLAY

Francis Jarman

THE BORGO PRESS
An Imprint of Wildside Press
Rockville, Maryland

MMVII

First published in Germany in 2001
by Books on Demand GmbH, Norderstedt

Cover graphic by Titus Twister

Copyright © 2001, 2007 by Francis Jarman

All rights reserved. No part of this book may be reproduced in any form without the expressed written consent of the publisher. All performance rights are reserved by the author.

THIS EDITION FIRST PUBLISHED IN 2007

AUTHOR'S NOTE

Like my earlier plays *A Star Fell* (1998) and *Girls Will Be Girls* (2000), *Lip Service* was written specially for the English Drama Group at Hildesheim University. During rehearsals, the plot was changed, new scenes were evolved and some old ones cut, text material was added (especially jokes and gags) and one or two of the characters underwent a process of reinterpretation. Everyone contributed something, but I would particularly like to thank the director, Paul Willin; Burkhard Schäfer and Olaf Schulz; and Titus Twister and the hardworking video group. A few additional changes have been made for this new international edition of the text.

– Francis Jarman

CHARACTERS

- At Cosfem:

Arabella Merchant (Bella), *Chief Executive*
Melanie, *Finance*
Candida, *Marketing*
Sylvia, *Personnel*
Julia Johnson, *Public Relations*
Miss Lavinia Casket, *a secretary*
Desmond Barrow, *a secretary (and writer)*
Joanna, *a camerawoman*

- Visitors:

Patrick, *a job applicant*
Charlene, *a film actress*
Jean-Pierre Lamour, *a film actor*
Rick O'Toole, *a singer*
Bill Bullock, *founder of Bullock's Active Marketing*

- Video/TV:

Dave Richards, *a TV commentator*
Frank Bigelow, *a TV interviewer*
First 'Young Event' wannabe (boring)
Second 'Young Event' wannabe (enthusiastic)
Third 'Young Event' wannabe (sexy)
'Young Event' actress
'Young Event' actor

The play is set in the headquarters of the cosmetics company Cosfem.

Lip Service was first presented in the Auditorium Maximum of Hildesheim University on June 19th, 2001 by the English Drama Group of the University with the following cast:

Arabella Merchant (Bella)	**Hanna Barst**
Melanie	**Cora Steigenberger**
Candida	**Heike Stamer**
Sylvia	**Kerstin Bischoff**
Julia Johnson	**Katharina Bovermann**
Miss Lavinia Casket	**Jenny Richmond**
Desmond Barrow	**Burkhard Schäfer**
Joanna	**Sonja-Maria Klauß**
Patrick	**Johannes Sieland**
Charlene	**Christine Pahlmann**
Jean-Pierre Lamour	**Thomas Wilhelm**
Rick O'Toole	**Tom Zielen**
Bill Bullock	**Christian Friedrich**
Dave Richards	**David Heinemann**
Frank Bigelow	**Felix Oelmann**
Boring 'Young Event' wannabe	**Monika Marschall**
Enthusiastic 'Young Event' wannabe	**Simone Brandes**
Sexy 'Young Event' wannabe	**Asal Dardan**
'Young Event' actress	**Nina Riedel**
'Young Event' actor	**Andreas Gust**

and

Michaela Aue, **Valerie Baucke**, **He Yilin**, **Ulrike Michiels**, **Matthias Müller**, **Hanno Raichle**, **Christina Richter**, **Olaf Schulz**, **Julia Schönleiter**, **Iván Valerón** and **Christoph** ('Dr. Beast') **Werner**

Video Production	**Titus Twister**
Production Manager	**Matthias Müller**
Director	**Paul Willin**

PART ONE

[video]

A clip from a TV news report.

COMMENTATOR. And one final item of business news today comes from a medium-sized company that has never hit the headlines before, although its products are well-known to the public. Here is a clue.

CHARLENE *[oozingly].*
                    I am a woman.
In the life of a woman ... *[Brandishing a lipstick]*
                    there are events.
There are events in which a woman is most a woman.
There are events in which a woman is most herself.

INTERVIEWER. Yes, the famous Charlene, with a product made by Cosfem, 'cosmetics *for* women *by* women'. Cosfem is a family enterprise, but with an interesting difference – the feminist touch. Now Cosfem has a new Chief Executive Officer, Arabella Merchant, who is committed to making the company a major force not only here in Britain but internationally as well. Frank Bigelow spoke to Arabella Merchant earlier this morning.

> **BELLA.** You're right, it won't be easy, and if we have to break a few eggs to make the omelette, we will!

INTERVIEWER. Cosfem is a company with an unusual profile.

BELLA. We make products for women. We *are* women.

INTERVIEWER. So there are no men working for Cosfem?

BELLA *[laughing unpleasantly].*
Well, just as some very famous companies have one token woman working at a senior level, Cosfem has a token man. And do you know what he does? He's a typist! That's our little joke.

INTERVIEWER. Cosfem, a company that will soon be going places under dynamic new management. Remember the name. This is one to watch. This is Frank Bigelow with our business update, and now back to Dave Richards in the studio.

Fade to black.

[1]

The main office. Sitting round a long table in conference are: BELLA, CANDIDA, MELANIE *and* SYLVIA; MISS CASKET *is taking notes.*

SYLVIA. *I* still think that that came over very well. Well done Candida, we haven't been on the news for a long time!

CANDIDA *[surprised, then ironical]*. Thank you, Sylvia. It's nice to hear the Personnel Department expressing opinions on Marketing. You're quite sure you don't want to take over Marketing altogether?

MELANIE *[enthusiastically]*. No no, Candida, as long as Sylvia's opinions are constructive …

CANDIDA. But I'm surprised to find Sylvia in agreement with me. *[To* SYLVIA*]* Have we ever agreed on *anything* before?

MELANIE *[gushingly]*. Oh, this is wonderful! It's so heartwarming! This is how it *should* be! Sisters should be partners, not opponents. *[Noticing that the others haven't really understood her]* I mean sisters in the feminist sense, of course.

CANDIDA *[to* SYLVIA*]*. One thing is certain, though, *[To the others, cattily]* if even *Sylvia* likes it, it must be getting through to a *very* broad consumer base. How could we describe it? The lowest common denominator? We're obviously aiming at the mass market now!

BELLA *[explosively]*. Oh, just shut up! It is *crap*! *[Pause]* When I took over this company three weeks ago – for crisis management – I was told that it was full of idiots. That was an understatement! Just think of some of the recent 'successes': 'Tasty Lips – the Lipstick with that special taste.' O.K., you might think. A new direction. But – cheese and onion? Salt and vinegar? Fried chicken and garlic?! I ask you! And what was the *next* great brainwave? Honey-flavoured lipstick – with real honey! 200 wretched people stung by wasps ...

MELANIE *[helpfully]*. 264.

BELLA.... and who had to pay the hospital bills? But it gets even better, doesn't it? 'Spray Lips – the spray-on lipstick for the woman in a hurry.' Sure – great – if you want to walk round looking like Coco the Clown. And the names, godammit. *That much [Appropriate gesture with finger and thumb]* market research would have told you that a lipstick called 'Mist' wouldn't be a hit on the *German* market! Even a peek in the dictionary would have helped. *'Mist*: Rubbish, nonsense trash; alternatively: animal droppings, dung, manure.' Oh, brilliant! *[Quickly pointing her finger threateningly at* SYLVIA, *who was about to say something]* No, not a word! *[Pause]* And as for the ad, it was a disaster. The whole feature was useless. The commentary was useless. And that *woman* in the advertisement ...

MELANIE *[helpfully again]*. Charlene.

BELLA *[looking at* CANDIDA*]*. ... we don't need to ask who found *her* for us! In what graveyard of

Hollywood has-beens did you dig *her* up? Wasn't she in *Gone With the Wind* – the silent version?

MELANIE *[waving what looks like a contract]*. But we *have* to use her. She's famous. And she has an exclusive contract for five years.

BELLA *[to* CANDIDA, *venomously]*. Are you sure she'll even live that long? *[Struggling to keep her fury under control]* O.K., so we're stuck with the bitch. I had a look at the whole advertisement. What is the rubbish *about*? Where's the context? What are these *events* the woman keeps on talking about?

CANDIDA. That's the product-name.

BELLA *[to* CANDIDA*]*. You again! You've done enough damage! How can anyone be so *thick*? I know very well what products this company sells – I *run* it! But *you* won't be part of it for much longer, my dear, I can see that coming. *[To the whole group]* And you won't be the only one! I've already fired half a dozen people in this company, and that isn't the end of the story! Ladies, you know the score – this firm hasn't turned in a profit for years now. If we don't come up with a convincing new ad campaign for the shareholder conference – and come up with it fast, the whole joint gets sold off to Elizabeth-bloody-Arden. And that means ALL your jobs!

MELANIE. My grandmother wouldn't sell her shares. Cosfem has always been a family firm. It would absolutely break her heart.

CANDIDA. Don't be silly, Melanie. Your granny might own a massive slice of the pie, but if the rest of the shareholders vote for the merger, we're screwed.

SYLVIA. And I always thought *[With a vulgar grin]* that you *enjoyed* being screwed, Candida ...

BELLA. We've only got *two days* left - could we get back to the topic at hand, please? So, you tell me – what *are* these 'events' that the ageing Hollywood lady is trying to tell us about? Is she going to the Olympics? Is she about to have a menopausal flush? Is she going to become a grandmother? *[Holding up the lipstick]* And why is she alone with *this*? No, I guess I don't want to know! *[Decisively]* There has to be someone else in the spot with her – give the whole thing a bit of taste – and I don't mean cheese and onion.

MELANIE. I thought that we could, er ... *[Looking spitefully at* CANDIDA*]* – and I said so at the time, but nobody listened! – *[To the whole group once again]* I thought that we could, er, use a second woman, you know, create a scene – an *event*! – of sisterly tenderness ...

BELLA *[looking heavenwards]*. And I thought that I'd heard it all – God give me patience! *[To* MELANIE, *sarcastically]* Darling, I know that this is not really your scene, but why *do* women wear makeup? Quote.

'Women ... wear makeup ... so that men ... will notice them!' Unquote. *[Looking nastily at* CANDIDA*]* Or, in some cases, *think* that men will notice them! *[To herself]* Ah, why do I bother? *[To the whole group].* Ten minutes break! *I* shall go to the ladies', *you* will come up with a name, a *man's* name, please, some appropriate gigolo to play opposite our beauty queen in the new version of the ad *which is to be filmed immediately.* Do I make myself clear? Do-not-waste-my-time. My time is too valuable. Find that man quickly or *[Emphatically]* – heads will roll!

MISS CASKET *[as everyone starts to get up].* Pardon my asking, but did you want the coffee and biscuits served after the break or at the end of the meeting?

BELLA *[to* MELANIE*].* Who is this person? Do we have a reason for employing her? *[Then turning to* SYLVIA*]* The Personnel Department ought to know, surely?

MELANIE. It's Miss Casket, the secretary.

BELLA. Someone deal with it, please – I don't wish to be bothered with stupid details. Or stupid people. Tell the woman how to do her job properly or get rid of her. *[To the whole group]* Ten minutes, ladies, and then I want a name.

Enter JULIA *in a great rush and very out of breath.*

JULIA *[offering* BELLA *her hand].* Julia Johnson,

Public Relations, we haven't met yet, I've just come back from my holidays!

BELLA [*ignoring* JULIA*'s outstretched hand*].
Ten minutes. I want a name. Or else! [*Exit*]

JULIA [*puzzled*]. Was it something I said?

CANDIDA *and* MELANIE *start to move off after* BELLA.

CANDIDA [*a parting shot to* SYLVIA]. *I* have a name!

SYLVIA [*not impressed*]. Er, Candida, wasn't it?

CANDIDA. Very funny, ha-ha-ha. Have *you* got a name? Bad luck if you haven't, darling. Let's see who still has a job tomorrow! [*Exeunt* CANDIDA *and* MELANIE]

JULIA [*to* SYLVIA]. What did she mean by that? [*Chasing after* CANDIDA *and* MELANIE] Candida, what did you mean by that? What's all that about names? [*Exit*]

MISS CASKET [*deeply offended*]. I've worked for this company much longer than any of *you* have …

SYLVIA [*reassuringly*]. Don't worry about it, Lavinia.

MISS CASKET [*deeply offended*]. She's an evil woman. She's got no heart. She's got no manners. The way that she got rid of poor old Mr. Donaldson. And

Janet. And Dorothy and the others ...

SYLVIA. Yes, that was very brutal, with Janet and all of them. Don't worry, though, *you're* not really in danger. It's Candida she'll go for next. Or me, perhaps. And don't worry about the coffee, either. Leave it in the office next door. I doubt if *she'll* want any. She probably drinks blood.

MISS CASKET *[suddenly]*. Oh, I completely forgot. Office next door! There's someone waiting to see you. Wants to apply for that job as your assistant. *[Pause]* Janet's job. *[Pause]* Quite nice.

SYLVIA. The other women who applied were terrible ... Well, bring her in.

MISS CASKET. Not her, *him*. *[Exit]*

SYLVIA *[shocked, but also interested]*. Him?!

[2]

MISS CASKET *re-enters, leading in* **PATRICK**.

PATRICK. Hallo. My name's Patrick.

SYLVIA *[flippantly]*. Oh, someone else who's got a name!

PATRICK *[puzzled]*. I beg your pardon?

SYLVIA. Sorry, that was very rude – my mind was elsewhere. *[Friendly]* Hallo, I'm Sylvia. Look, I think I know why you're here, and I'm afraid you're wasting your time.

PATRICK *[surprised]*. I hope not. I've come about the job you advertised. I've got quite a lot of experience in personnel. *[He hands her his CV]*

SYLVIA *[browsing through it]*. Yes, you really have … but you're still wasting your time.

MISS CASKET. You'll excuse me, Sylvia. *[Moving towards the door]*

CANDIDA *re-enters, looking for something, and bumps into* MISS CASKET.

CANDIDA *[as* MISS CASKET *exits]*. Mind where you're going! Where did I put my file? *[Staring lustfully at* PATRICK*]* God, Sylvia, you *do* like them young! He *is* tasty! Is he from Rent-A-Boy? You can send him down to *my* office if you can't find a use for him! *[She finds her file and exits again]*

PATRICK. Did she mean what I think she meant?

SYLVIA *[laughing]*. Ah … um … she can be rather direct sometimes. But look, I can't give you a job, and nor can she – at least not an *office* job.

PATRICK. Why not?

SYLVIA *[after a pause]*. Do you know the *name* of this company?

PATRICK. Cosfem.

SYLVIA. Yes, Cosfem. 'Cosmetics *for* women *by* women.' *[Pause]* We don't really employ *men*. Although – we've got a man starting tomorrow as a typist, but that's just a sort of joke, you know, the token man? Basically it's the policy of the company not to employ men at any higher level of responsibility.

PATRICK. Is that legal?

SYLVIA. How do you mean?

PATRICK. Well, surely it wouldn't be legal if a company refused to employ *women*? Especially if the women who applied were better than any of the men. I bet I know a lot more about makeup than most women do!

SYLVIA. Yes, but in the world of employment men don't need this sort of legal protection. Men aren't discriminated against in the way that women are.

PATRICK. I'm a man, and I'm being discriminated against right now!

SYLVIA *[glancing at his CV]*. Um … Patrick … it's been nice talking to you, and if you were a woman, with *these* qualifications *[She hands him back his CV]* I'd give you the job immediately. Believe you me, I have *nothing* against men! But we have a new Chief Executive, Bella …

PATRICK. Yes, Arabella Merchant.

SYLVIA. My, you *have* done your homework! *[Confidentially]* Bella doesn't like men. I don't think she likes *people*. She sacked two people on the first day she was here and she's been doing it ever since – like the Queen of Hearts, 'Off with her head …!' *[Pause]* Look, if you're unhappy about this you could try talking to someone else. Melanie, perhaps, she's the number two, and her grandmother owns half the company … *[Then dismissing the idea]* No, forget it, that wouldn't work, I don't think Melanie *[With a gesture suggesting that* MELANIE *is slightly gaga]* lives on Planet Earth much of the time … I'm sorry, I really am! *[Looking at her watch]* I have to go now. Our meeting's going to restart, and I need a couple of minutes to think up a few names. Otherwise they may be advertising *my* job as well!

PATRICK. Names? You seem rather obsessed with names.

SYLVIA. Sorry, Patrick. Yes, I'm looking for a name. We need a sexy bloke – not too young! – for our TV advertising. Got any suggestions?

PATRICK. Hmm *[Thinks]* … I have, actually. Do you

know Rick O'Toole?

SYLVIA. The pop singer? 'Mister Sex'? The guy who insured his hips for a million dollars?

PATRICK. Believe it or not: He's my uncle!

SYLVIA. Really??! What a good idea! He would be great, just the right age, too. *[Cunning]* And he's just the type that Candida likes. Thanks for the tip! *[Seriously]* But I'm afraid I still can't offer you a job.

PATRICK. No, fair enough. *[Pause]* Actually, it's not fair at all. *[Pause]* Hey, look, my cousin needs a job, too. And her qualifications are even better than mine.

SYLVIA. Well, then, send her along. Now, if you'll excuse me ... *[She leads him out]*

Brief fade.

[3]

Re-enter BELLA, CANDIDA, MELANIE *and* MISS CASKET. *They take their seats.*

CANDIDA *[leering at* PATRICK *as he goes out]*. Not bad at all! Nice bum!

SYLVIA *[as she comes back in again and sits down]*. Just a man who wanted a job. Not much point coming to us, though ...

CANDIDA. What a pity...

BELLA *[ignoring this]*. Alright, ladies, give me names. Melanie? *[With a dismissive gesture]* No, you obviously don't know any men! Not that kind, anyway. Candida? I'm sure that *you* know plenty ...

CANDIDA. There is an obvious name.

BELLA *[beaming nastily at her]*. Good. I knew we could rely on you when it comes to men. But it had better be a *good* name.

Enter JULIA, *quite out of breath.*

JULIA. Dear oh me, late again! Sorry folks, so much to do, so little time to do it!

MELANIE *[in a loud whisper]*. Try to make an effort!

BELLA *[glaring]*. Who are you? Do you work here?

JULIA *[offering* BELLA *her hand once again]*. Julia Johnson, Public Relations, delighted to meet you!

BELLA *[still glaring, and refusing the hand]*. Why should you be? *[Ominously]* You don't *know* me yet. Now sit down and shut up! *[To* CANDIDA*]* You were saying?

CANDIDA *[preeningly]*. While *other* people were sitting on their backsides drinking coffee *[Triumphant grin at* SYLVIA*]* I made a few quick calls to contacts of mine in the entertainment business and I think that, once again, Candida has come up with the right answer.

BELLA *[impatient]*. Yes, yes, go on!

JULIA*'s mobile phone goes off with a ridiculously loud and stupid signal.*

JULIA *[grinning, embarrassed]*. Oops, naughty me! *[Answering the phone as she walks out]* Johnson! Julia! P-R! *[Pause]* No! *[Pause]* Yes? *[Pause]* No!! *[Pause]* Yes? [She glances at* BELLA *who is glaring at her and so she goes out,* BELLA, MELANIE *and* CANDIDA *glaring at her]*

CANDIDA. As I was saying …

BELLA *[extremely impatient]*. Yes, please go on.

JULIA *[re-entering and finishing her telephone conversation]*. Look, just give it to Joanna, O.K.? She always knows what to do. *[Turning to the others, with a beaming smile]* Ah, the world of high technology! A closed book to the non-specialist! But everything is under control!

MELANIE. I didn't realise you were in charge of the laboratories, Julia, I thought you did Public Relations.

JULIA *[still grinning]*. Oh, that's just our cameraman. He can't get the silly camera started! Joanna's on her way, she'll fix it.

CANDIDA *[quickly, before* **BELLA** *has time to explode]*. As I was saying ...

BELLA *[interrupting her]*. When the camera is working, I want some shots for the new junior line. 'Young Event'. Especially the lipstick. Take the camera out on the street. We need some juvenile delinquent as 'The Face of Young Event'. Some student or shopgirl. Thin. vacuous expression. Rubbish like that. *[Quickly]* Nothing pimply, though! Now, go on, Candida. *[Glaring pointedly at* JULIA*]* Before I lose my patience ...

CANDIDA. He's just right for this, but we can't approach him directly, we'll have to do this through his agent, Bill Bullock. You know, Bullock's Active Marketing.

JULIA *[loudly, and with a punching gesture]*. Bam!

MELANIE *[jumping out of her skin]*. What?

CANDIDA. Julia's little joke. You know? Bullock's – Active – Marketing spells: BAM.

JULIA *[again]*. Bam! *[Apologetically]* Sorry. I used to know Bill at university. I see him in the pub sometimes. He's a complete wally. Sylvia knows him too. That 'Bam!' trick is something that *he* does.

MISS CASKET. Still, it could have been worse. Bullock's *Universal* Marketing, for example.

JULIA. B-U-M. That describes Bill's character quite well.

BELLA. Ladies, can we get to the point, please! Candida, what's the man's *name*?

CANDIDA. He's ultra-smooth. He's magnetic. Women will kill themselves for him. He's simply oozing with sex appeal. He's a *god*. He's unbelievable. They call him 'Mister Irresistible' …

Enter JOANNA.

JOANNA *[to* JULIA*].* Candida talking about sex again? Hallo Julia, you coming? I've got the camera started, I'm afraid Harry's been at the bottle again – he was trying to squeeze an audio tape into the video camera. But I've sorted it out.

JULIA. You're a treasure, Joanna. Be right with you! *[Exit* JOANNA. *Leaping up]* So, the call of duty! 'Young Event' – here we come! Away, away! *[Exit]*

BELLA *[to* MELANIE*].* Remind me to have a look at that woman's contract sometime soon. *[To* CANDIDA*]* Now, Candida: *the name*?

CANDIDA *[theatrically]*. Jean-Pierre Lamour!

BELLA *[without a clue]*. Jean-Pierre Lamour?

CANDIDA. Jean-Pierre Lamour! 'The Master of a Thousand Romantic Moments.' The French Cary Grant. The Gallic Gable. *[Dramatically]* 'The Man Whose Name is Love!'

SYLVIA *[pretending to be helpful]*. My parents used to like his films. When I was small. They were on the telly on Sunday afternoons. But I think he's from Manchester.

CANDIDA *[desperate]*. The *style* is Gallic! And he's done loads of films with Charlene. He's done *love scenes* with her.

SYLVIA. God, he must be a brave man!

CANDIDA *[final attempt]*. And he needs the money.

BELLA *[to* CANDIDA*]*. O.K. Get him! But don't spend too much.

CANDIDA *[glowing]*. He and Bill Bullock are gonna be here tomorrow, first thing in the morning! And Charlene will be here as well! Things are gonna be exploding around here!

BELLA. Well done, Candida. Keep up the good work – at this rate, you might even get to keep your job!

[Looking around] I take it that there are no other candidates? Sylvia?

SYLVIA. Well, since you come to mention it ... what about Rick O'Toole?

BELLA. Is he another of these geriatric showstars?

CANDIDA *[with unexpected intensity]*. No, Rick O'Toole has got a lot of style.

SYLVIA. He's got something that appeals to women *of a certain age*! *[Spiteful grin at* CANDIDA*]*

BELLA. Then get him, too. We'll try them both out with Charlene. *[Getting up]* Melanie, come with me, we've wasted enough time. *[Noticing* MISS CASKET *clearing up the papers left on the table]* What is that awful woman doing? Give her some proper work to do or throw her out! *[*MELANIE *whispers something to* MISS CASKET, *who leaves in a great huff. Exeunt* BELLA *and* MELANIE*]*

[4]

CANDIDA *[thoughtfully]*. That was very clever, Sylvia, trying to upstage me like that. I've underestimated you, haven't I? But I won't make *that* mistake again.

SYLVIA *[with pretend naivety]*. Just trying to be

helpful, Candida. We're not at war!

CANDIDA. Oh yes we are. That woman is a killer. You heard what she said. Whatever happens at that shareholder conference, more jobs are going to go. And it won't be bloody Melanie, will it? So I want to make sure that it's not *me*.

SYLVIA. Well, I would guess that Julia ...

CANDIDA *[interrupting her]*. Julia doesn't count! She doesn't give a toss. She's got snobby friends everywhere, she'd get a new job straightaway. But *I* wouldn't ...

SYLVIA. Nor would I.

CANDIDA. Bella likes hurting people. So it won't be Julia she goes for. It'll be someone like you or me.

SYLVIA. Can't we work together on this?

CANDIDA *[ignoring this offer]*. It was good timing, too. You had your candidate all ready and waiting to spoil my little moment of glory! And what a clever choice. Rick O'Toole! I've always liked him. But I'll tell you something, darling. This time you've got it wrong. He's not right for this campaign, believe me. *[Warming to her subject]* And what a *waste* it would be to have him playing around with *Charlene* in front of the cameras. Such a virile man! But do invite him by all means. I look forward to meeting him tomorrow!

Exeunt. Fade to black.

[video]

A take for 'Young Event':

'YOUNG EVENT' WANNABE 1 *[reading in a droning voice].*
> Hey, cool, when he looks at me
> I wanna know
> At moments like this
> I wanna be *in control*
> Me and my lipstick
> Are goin' somewhere
> The rest of the world
> Had better take care!
> *Young Event [Holding up the lipstick without much enthusiasm]* – what every girl needs!
> That O.K.?

JOANNA *[off-camera].* No, that was pathetic. Never mind. And the next!

Another take for 'Young Event':

'YOUNG EVENT' WANNABE 2 *[this time over-enthusiastic].*
> Hey, cool, when he looks at me
> I wanna know

At moments like this
I wanna be *in control*
Me and my lipstick
Are goin' somewhere
The rest of the world
Had better take care!
Young Event [Brandishing the lipstick very dramatically] – what every girl needs!
That was alright, wasn't it?

JOANNA *[off-camera]*. Perhaps at half the speed, dear. And you don't need to stab the camera with it. We'll cut there.

Another take for 'Young Event':

'YOUNG EVENT' WANNABE 3 *[this time pouting and lascivious]*.
Hey, cool, when he looks at me
I wanna know
At moments like this
I wanna be *in control*
Me and my lipstick
Are goin' somewhere
The rest of the world
Had better take care!
Young Event [Thrusting the lipstick suggestively at the camera] – what every girl needs!
Hey, shouldn't I be doin' this with a fella?

JOANNA *[off-camera]*. I'm sure you will, sweetheart – quite soon! Look, could somebody open the window please? It's getting a bit steamy in here …

Fade to black.

[5]

The lights come up to reveal SYLVIA. *She is fiddling with a video recorder. Enter* CANDIDA, *holding a coffee mug.*

CANDIDA. Morning! Oh, been taping some home movies? What's his name, then? Mind if I have a look?

SYLVIA. Very funny, dearest. And good morning to you too. No, I've just been looking at what Joanna and Julia recorded for 'Young Event' yesterday. Less said, the better.

CANDIDA. Oh dear.

SYLVIA. But today it's the big guns. Charlene and Co. When are our candidates supposed to arrive?

CANDIDA. Any time now. Heavens, I'd better check my make-up. *[As* CANDIDA *moves off, she collides with* MISS CASKET *on her way in, leading* DESMOND*]* You awful woman, look where you're going! And what do you want? And who is that?

MISS CASKET. This is the new typist. Mr. …. er,

um… sorry? I didn't catch your name.

DESMOND *[brightly]*. My name's Desmond actually.

CANDIDA. Desmond Actually?

DESMOND. Well, it's actually *Desmond*.

CANDIDA. Actually Desmond or Desmond Actually? You don't seem to know what your own name is.

SYLVIA. Candida, don't be tiresome. I think you'll find that his name is Mr. Desmond Barrow. *[To* DESMOND*]* That's right, isn't it?

DESMOND *[gratefully]*. Oh thank you so much!

CANDIDA. Well, why didn't you say so, then? You're the token man, I suppose? *[To* SYLVIA*]* Token idiot, more like it. *[To* DESMOND*]* The typist?

DESMOND. Now, actually …

SYLVIA. Don't start that again!

DESMOND. … I'm a writer!

CANDIDA. Yes, but we didn't advertise for a writer, did we?

DESMOND. That's true, but I, er, sort of … want the job as a typist. *[Embarrassed]* I *need* the job. I've had a little … er … bad luck lately. I wrote this book, you see – *Barrow's Business Guide: 10 steps to financial success.*

SYLVIA. And?

DESMOND. I sold ten copies … So I went back to writing novels.

SYLVIA *[with sympathy]*. Writers don't earn very much, do they?

DESMOND. I've also got a little bookshop, you see. It's very nice, very quiet. Well, *of course* it's quiet, there are no customers! And that's why I had to look for a job. *[Recovering]* But it's not *just* the money. Actually, … Oh, sorry! Well, I'm also hoping for some material, some inspiration for a new novel. We writers tend to get stuck, up there in the ivory tower. So I said to myself: Desmond, it's time that you reminded yourself what real life is all about. And *that's* why I applied!

CANDIDA. Yes, yes, but can you do the job? Can you type?

DESMOND *[making very unconvincing typing gestures with just one or two fingers]*. Ah, well, I typed my last novel … Hundreds of pages in manuscript. Took me absolutely ages.

CANDIDA *[looking at him sceptically]*. Yes …

[Pause] Shorthand?

DESMOND *[looking at his hands, jokingly]*. No, quite normal. I take after my mother, you know.

CANDIDA. We do a lot of dictating around here ...

DESMOND *[smiling in the direction of* MISS CASKET*]*. Dictating? No, I can't believe that! Everyone's been so *nice* to me so far.

CANDIDA. This is getting weird! Look, do you use Word? Or Word Perfect?

DESMOND. I've used both of them. Now that you mention it, have you ever thought about the names? *Words* are what we writers use all the time ... And the *perfect* word is what we always hope to find. Who would have guessed that software companies could be so poetic? But I've always felt that the name 'Microsoft' has a poetic ring to it...

CANDIDA *[trying to concentrate]*. Excel?

DESMOND. I *try* to excel, but the publishers haven't discovered my work yet. Well, they have *discovered* it, but they always send the manuscripts back. But I haven't given up, oh no.

CANDIDA. And I thought I'd seen it all ... Token man, eh? Sylvia darling, I think I'll leave *this one* to you. *[She tries to brush past* MISS CASKET *but finds the* *secretary planted firmly in her path]* Oh for godssake what is it now?

MISS CASKET *[firmly]*. I just wanted to say that there are some visitors, too …

CANDIDA *[irritated]*. Don't pester me with any more things. *Personnel* looks after people. Visitors *are* people, aren't they, Sylvia? So Personnel can look after them. That's *your* job. For the time being, at least. *[To* MISS CASKET*]* And now get out of my way! *[Exit]*

MISS CASKET. But they're *her* visitors. And one of them is *very* charming. A French gentleman.. The other one may be an acquired taste. Shall I …?

SYLVIA. Show them in, Lavinia. And then you had better get Desmond organised. Teach him a few office skills. You'll like it here, Desmond. Not everyone's mad, but we're working on it!

MISS CASKET *[to* DESMOND*]*. Wheel this way, please, Mr. Barrow.

DESMOND. Oh, I like your sense of humour! Do call me Desmond, though. Everyone's been so nice, I'm sure that I'm going to love it here…

Exeunt MISS CASKET *and* DESMOND. MISS CASKET *returns leading* JEAN-PIERRE *and* BILL.

JEAN-PIERRE *[bowing exaggeratedly to* SYLVIA*]*. *Mon dieu*! A vision of loveliness! Like a man thirstin' in the desert, who sees not *one* mirage of an oasis on the 'orizon *[With a gesture towards* MISS CASKET*]*, but *two*! Jean-Pierre Lamour, at your service – in every possible way!

BILL. Hallo, Sylvia, long time, no see! And you haven't changed a bit – still the cutie of the campus *[Leering]* that we all knew and *loved*.

SYLVIA. Actually, Bill, *I* grew up.

BILL. Oh, nasty, nasty! What a wicked girl! But I gather that you want to do Big Business with Bill. *[Gesturing towards* JEAN-PIERRE*]* He may be slimy, but he's all mine! You want him, you pay!

SYLVIA *[to* JEAN-PIERRE*]*. Hallo, Monsieur Lamour. Actually, I know you're from Manchester, so you can drop the French *accent* until we get to the filming, O.K.?

JEAN-PIERRE. Not Manchester, darling, *Wilmslow*. Much better class. *[To* MISS CASKET*]* I 'ope that we will 'ave the *plaisir* of workin' together, *ma chérie*?

SYLVIA. I'll go and tell people that you've arrived. *[To* MISS CASKET*]* Lavinia, you better come too. I don't think it's safe for you to be with Monsieur Lamour without a chaperone!

MISS CASKET *[disappointed]*. Oh, what a pity!

JEAN-PIERRE *[as* SYLVIA *and* MISS CASKET *exeunt]. Au revoir, ma petite!* *[To* BILL*]* Ah, *les femmes*, what can one say?

BILL *[charmlessly]*. It's so easy with women – you look at them, and they fall into your lap!

JEAN-PIERRE. No, Bill, that is not true. This delicious little apple *[Gesturing in the direction in which* MISS CASKET *left]* will fall into Jean-Pierre's lap because the fruit is ripe, is burstin' with juice, and because Jean-Pierre understands and loves the fruits of the garden.

BILL. Come on, I don't believe a word of it! This place is full of crumpet, and I could have *any* of them if I wanted to!

JEAN-PIERRE. No, Bill, with all due respect … You are a nice boy, you 'ave potential. But, no …

BILL. They want a young bloke.

JEAN-PIERRE. No, Bill, they want experience. And maturity.

BILL. They want a young bloke. They want muscle… in places *where it counts*. You wait and see!

JEAN-PIERRE *[suddenly very serious]*. Bill – don't do

anything stupid! Just stay focused, alright? I'm getting old. I need this job. But promise me that it won't be like the other ones! No more standing outside supermarkets in the rain, please! No more TV marketing, no more pantomime horses!

[6]

Enter CHARLENE, *moving rather uncertainly and myopically about the stage.*

CHARLENE. Hallo-ee!

JEAN-PIERRE *[to* CHARLENE*]*. No! It cannot be! Surely not? *Merveilleuse!*

CHARLENE *[staggering towards* BILL*]*. Is that you, Jean-Pierre?

JEAN-PIERRE. Yes, but I am over 'ere! 'Ave you forgotten your contact lenses again? *[Grasping her passionately as she almost misses him completely]* Charlene!

CHARLENE. Jean-Pierre! *[Conspiratorially]* I left the bloody things at home. You know how I hate them!

JEAN-PIERRE. But can you see anythin' without them?

CHARLENE. Well, people can see *me*, can't they? Isn't

that enough? Anyway, I can't wear them for shooting. Every time there's a romantic scene ...

JEAN-PIERRE *[moving closer to her]*. And *all* scenes with you are romantic scenes.

CHARLENE *[ignoring his flattery]*. Every time there's a romantic scene, and the camera goes in close, my eyes look like the surface of a cold rice-pudding.

JEAN-PIERRE. Delicious to eat?

CHARLENE. No, glazed over and sticky-looking!

BILL *[coughing discreetly]*. A-hem.

CHARLENE *[noticing him for the first time, but unable to see him clearly]*. Is that the cameraman?

BILL *[almost knocking her over]*. Hi! I'm Bill – from BAM!

CHARLENE *[jumping out of her skin]*. I'm not deaf, you know! *[Peering at him]* Are you a student? I didn't know students could get this kind of job.

BILL. No, no, I'm not a student. Why do you ask?

CHARLENE. Well why are you wearing running shoes?

BILL. No, these aren't running shoes, they're sneakers.

They're very expensive. You must have seen them before? They're absolutely the latest! 'Big Bang – everything started with Big Bang!' Now, *there's* a nice marketing line! Wish we had their account. Bit too big for BAM. BAM! That's my company. Bullock's Active Marketing. I'm Bullock!

CHARLENE. Oh, Mr. Bullock is your father? Must be nice working for him in the student holidays!

BILL. Er, no ... I'm not a student.

CHARLENE. But if you want to get a proper job with him later, I'm sure he'll tell you to wear proper shoes. Proper men always wear real polished leather shoes. Ah, proper men! Where *are* they in this day and age! *[*JEAN-PIERRE, *grinning, gives* BILL *a thumbs-down signal behind* CHARLENE*'s back. Peering again]* Jean-Pierre?

JEAN-PIERRE. You gorgeous creature!

CHARLENE *[throwing herself at* JEAN-PIERRE, *as* BILL *makes a gesture of frustration]*. It's been so long! A real man – at last!

JEAN-PIERRE. Sorry, Bill! *[But then to* CHARLENE*]* Oh, *chérie,* please mind my back!

CHARLENE. I can't wait to start filming! *[Peering for him again]* Jean-Pierre? Are you alright?

JEAN-PIERRE *[unconvincingly]*.
It's a tennis injury – I must go easy on my fore'and!
And on my *service*!

[7]

Enter SYLVIA *and* RICK.

RICK. Did I hear a call for real men?

SYLVIA. You behave yourself, Mr. O'Toole, this is the competition!

RICK *[rushing across to* CHARLENE *and more or less knocking* JEAN-PIERRE *aside]*. No, no, this is Charlene – the one and only Charlene!

CHARLENE *[very pleased]*. I don't believe I've had the pleasure …?

RICK. O'Toole. Call me Rick. Pleasure is most definitely the word! We're going to have some great times, baby! *[Over his shoulder, to* SYLVIA*]* When does the filming start?

JEAN-PIERRE *[irritated]*. I 'aven't 'ad the pleasure either.

RICK. Hey, it's Jean-Pierre Lamour! I used to watch your films when I was a kid. Sexy, man, *really* sexy – even in black and white!

JEAN-PIERRE *[spitefully]*. But I thought you were younger, Mr. O'Toole? It's wonderful, what they can do with makeup these days!

RICK. Call me Rick! But we've met before, Jean-Pierre, don't you remember? I did a show up in Stockport – or some other place near Manchester with lots of factories – you come from round there, don't you?

JEAN-PIERRE. Don't waste your time, Rick. You won't get this job. They want a *kisser*. And *nobody* kisses like Jean-Pierre Lamour. *[To* CHARLENE*]* Isn't that right, *chérie*?

RICK. Kissing is only where it *starts*, baby. Big boys move on to the advanced stuff.

JEAN-PIERRE. We're 'ere to make a film, Rick. Nothing *primitif*. We're actors, professionals – some of us, at least …

RICK. I don't act, baby, I *am*. *[Giving* CHARLENE *a heavy look]* When I burn, I *burn*!

SYLVIA *[laughing]*. You gentlemen have sized up the situation very nicely! We only need *one* of you, but we'll try you both out with Charlene when the camera team gets here. Then we'll decide. Competition is the spice of life!

BILL *[pushing himself forward]*. But I understood that

it was my client who was being asked to take on this job?

RICK *[aggressively]*. Who are *you*, then?

BILL. Bullock! Bullock from BAM!

RICK *[threateningly]*. Look, Mr. – I must be careful to get your name right! – *Bullock*, my old friend Jean-Pierre here may be a bit long in the tooth but I don't think he needs some jumped-up little prat like *you* to do his talking for him!

SYLVIA. Now there's no need to be unpleasant to each other…

BILL. To avoid misunderstandings, I should point out that Jean-Pierre Lamour is exclusively, is *only* available through Bullock's Active Marketing!

RICK *[to* **SYLVIA***]*. That suits me! Then there's no need to go to any fuss, is there? Rick O'Toole is available here and now, you don't need an agent, you can do a deal with me *man to man*! Sorry, *woman* to man! *[To* **JEAN-PIERRE***]* Bad luck, Jean-Pierre, look's like you've come out of retirement for nothing!

SYLVIA. We haven't decided anything yet. In fact, we'll try out Mr. Lamour with Charlene first.

BILL *[triumphantly]*. And very sensible too, if you ask me. Save everybody a lot of time.

RICK *[to* **BILL***].* Don't push your luck, sonny!

Enter CANDIDA.

CANDIDA. Darlings, how gorgeous to see you! *Jean-Pierre! [There is some affected Gallic kissing]* Mwa! Mwa!

JEAN-PIERRE *[still with a stiff back].* I am dazzled! I am overwhelmed! *Ma petite*, I think you know my agent …

BILL *steps forward self-importantly but* CANDIDA *brushes straight past him.*

CANDIDA. It can't be! It *is*!!

RICK. Rick O'Toole. No more, no less.

CANDIDA *[glowing].* 'Mister Sex'!

RICK. Yes, there have been stories … *[He turns away from her for a moment, then wiggles his hips]* Much exaggerated, no doubt. But a man does what a man has to do.

CANDIDA *[still entranced].* Indeed, indeed.

RICK *[with mock coyness].* And there's not a single lady who's ever complained …

CHARLENE *[fascinated].* What a hunk!

JEAN-PIERRE *[very irritated at* CHARLENE*'s interest in* RICK*].* Charlene and I 'ave made many films together. *The Name of the Tulip.*

BILL. Great film, that one! Romantic historical drama. Lots of religion. Lots of … *[With an appropriate gesture]* *action.*

CHARLENE. I played the nun who gets raped.

JEAN-PIERRE. I was the rapist.

BILL. Something for everyone – a true family film!

JEAN-PIERRE. *All Quiet on the Eastern Front.*

BILL. Romantic war film. A film with a powerful message! Make love, not war.

CHARLENE. I played the prostitute.

BILL. You were a wonderful prostitute, those were great scenes!

JEAN-PIERRE. *Lassie the All-American Dog.*

RICK. Lassie?!

BILL. Romantic animal drama. A story straight from the heart.

RICK. So which of you played the dog?

CHARLENE. I was Lassie's owner. Jean-Pierre was the vet who had to put Lassie to sleep, because they thought she had been attacking cattle down on the ranch.

JEAN-PIERRE. There was a big love scene in the vet's surgery. I 'ad the needle in my 'and. But I couldn't do it! I looked into Lassie's eyes …

CHARLENE. … and then into mine …

JEAN-PIERRE. … and then the sheriff came with the order – Lassie was saved! It was deeply movin'.

BILL. That was a five-handkerchief film! Lassie got an Oscar nomination.

CHARLENE. And then there was *Casablanca*.

JEAN-PIERRE. Ah, *Casablanca*!

RICK [*amazed*]. *Casablanca*??

JEAN-PIERRE. Er, *Casablanca Part Two*. The remake.

RICK. Must've been before my time.

JEAN-PIERRE [*still irritated at* CHARLENE's *interest in* RICK]. But we 'ave to look a'ead to new challenges. I turned down several 'ollywood offers to be 'ere today. To recreate some of my greatest moments with

Charlene. I believe I 'eard someone say that Charlene and I would be on first, *n'est-ce pas?*

CANDIDA *[breaking out of her reverie].* Oh, yes. *[To* JEAN-PIERRE, BILL *and* CHARLENE*]* You three had better come along with me. Have a run through the text or something.

CHARLENE *[peering myopically in the direction of* RICK*].* What a pity – just when it was getting interesting! *[*JEAN-PIERRE *gives her a black look]*

Exeunt CANDIDA, JEAN-PIERRE, BILL *and* CHARLENE.

SYLVIA. What a delightful man. What a gentleman.

RICK *[contemptuously].* Well, he can still walk, I suppose. Just about. That's quite something at *his* age! *[Enter* MELANIE *and* JULIA. RICK *doesn't notice them at first]* And that Charlene, what a looker – I bet she goes like the clappers! *[Now seeing* MELANIE *and* JULIA; *to* JULIA*]* Oh, I beg your pardon.

JULIA. Don't mind me! *[Offering her hand]* Delighted. Julia, I/c P-R! You must be Rick O'Toole. Good that you're here. *[*JULIA*'s mobile phone goes off again]* Hi. *[Pause]* You don't say! *[Pause]* You don't say!! *[Pause]* You don't say!!!

SYLVIA. Who was that?

JULIA. I don't know – he didn't say. *[To* Rick*]* Well, must be off, I've got more people to film! First it was 'Young Event', now it's Charlene. Better late than never! Tally ho!

RICK. I'd like to take a look at this too, if I may – see if Jean-Pierre *[With a wiggle of the hips]* can still move all the parts that matter ...

JULIA. Be my guest!

Exeunt JULIA *and* RICK.

[8]

MELANIE *[collapsing onto a chair]*. I don't think I can take any more of this. Someone is doing this to me deliberately. Our company sets up a feminist policy, and then someone brings creatures like that into the building! This company is going downhill. They serve far too much meat in the canteen. And Sylvia, I must tell you something - *[In a confidential whisper]* did you know that there are *anatomical drawings* in the ladies' toilet on the third floor? Horrible, beastly things! No woman would draw anything like that.

SYLVIA. Oh, I'm not so sure about that ... *[Breezily]* What do they show?

MELANIE *[with a shudder]*. Unspeakable, unmentionable things. *[She whispers in* SYLVIA*'s ear]*

SYLVIA. And?

MELANIE *[shocked]*. What do you mean, *and*? Isn't that enough?

SYLVIA *[laughing]*. It wouldn't be enough for *me* on a Saturday night!

MELANIE. You're disgusting, Sylvia. Do you really think that you have a future in a feminist company?

SYLVIA. Come on, brighten up! And can't you cut down on the feminist ramblings once in a while?

MELANIE. You should really take our cause more seriously, Sylvia. Anyway, what I wanted to tell you – you're getting a new assistant, to replace Janet. Bella's just been interviewing her. A lovely girl, very sweet, very *pure*. I won't have her corrupted by that sort of talk.

SYLVIA. No, *of course* not! *[Pause]* Do I know this girl? I *am* the Personnel Manager. Aren't I supposed to do the interviewing?

MELANIE. You've met her cousin, she said.

SYLVIA. Ah, then that'll be Patrick's cousin! Well, that was quick.

MELANIE. I wish I could have offered the girl something in *my* department. Such innate femininity!

The kind of *spiritual beauty* that only another woman can truly appreciate.

Enter BELLA *and* PATRICK, *who is now dressed as a woman, 'Patricia'.*

BELLA. What a lot of nonsense you talk, Melanie, wittering on like that! Sylvia, this is your new assistant. She has excellent qualifications …

SYLVIA *[astounded]*. Oh!

BELLA. I beg your pardon?

SYLVIA. Sorry, just a bit surprised for a moment. I've already met Miss, er …

'PATRICIA'. Patricia.

SYLVIA. I've already met Miss Patricia's cousin Patrick.

BELLA. Yes, she told me. And why are you staring like that?

SYLVIA. Oh, um, it's just the uncanny resemblance between the cousins. More like twins!

'PATRICIA'. That's what everyone says.

BELLA *[to* SYLVIA*]*. I want the two of you working together efficiently. If she's no good, I'll sack her. If she's very good, I'll sack *you*. Quiet efficiency is what I want, O.K.?

SYLVIA [*offering* 'PATRICIA' *her hand*]. I'm sure we can work together. Haven't we already met, though?

'PATRICIA'. No, that was definitely Patrick that you met.

SYLVIA [*laughing*]. Oh, you're totally right about that! It *was* Patrick that I met! And how *is* Patrick, then?

BELLA [*interrupting*]. Great! That's how I like it, keep it up! In the long term, one of you will have to go, I suppose, but for the moment I want departmental harmony. [*About to go, then turning round and striking a pompous pose; what follows is a dictator-like speech*] Perhaps I haven't made myself clear. I see an international future for this company! And the name of that future: feminist cosmetics! 'Cosmetics *for* women *by* women.' There are a number of things you need to be aware of. We are a *team*. [*Sometime during the talk, when* BELLA *isn't looking,* SYLVIA *gives a military salute*] We have to work together. We need to develop a sense of group loyalty and team spirit! Do you understand what I mean?

'PATRICIA'. I think so.

SYLVIA [*in a whisper*]. You will soon enough!

BELLA *[giving* SYLVIA *a sharp look, then turning to* MELANIE*]*. Alright, Melanie, we've wasted enough time here. Show me those contracts again, there must be some way to save money on staff. And no Margaret Thatcher jokes when I'm out! *[Exit]*

MELANIE *[to* 'PATRICIA'*, with appropriate gesture]*. Bye-eee! *[Exit]*

[9]

SYLVIA *[mustering* 'PATRICIA' *up and down for a while, then:]*. So, *Patricia*, what's with the Tootsie act? Curiosity is killing me.

'PATRICIA' *[still pretending]*. I beg your pardon.

SYLVIA. Come on, Patrick, you don't fool *me*.

PATRICK. Well, I fooled *them*, didn't I?! What gave me away?

SYLVIA. Oh, just twenty-odd things, I guess. You didn't put on enough make-up to hide the Adam's apple. And then there's your walk, and … never mind, what's the point of all this?

PATRICK. They make all that fuss about 'men' and 'women', and they can't even tell the difference between them. I'm *me*, and I can do this job – and whether I'm a man or a woman doesn't matter.

Besides, I thought it would be a bit of a laugh.

SYLVIA. So you're here to take the piss out of us? Well, you might fool them for a while. They're all so preoccupied with their careers they can't see what's right here under their noses. *[Mustering him again]* Still, it's not bad, though.

PATRICK. I *told* you I knew all about makeup.

SYLVIA. How did you do the tits?

PATRICK. Oh, that was quite easy. You just have to know a little bit about hydraulics. *[Showing her]* This goes in here, and this fits in like that. They're rather nice, aren't they? Do you want to have a feel?

SYLVIA. They're bigger than mine. But I bet mine are more sensitive! *[Feeling his/her dress admiringly]* The dress is really good. Where'd you get it?

PATRICK *[quite flattered, but not in an affected manner]*. Funny you should say that! You know, there's this wonderful little store near Camden Market, and sometimes when I need a... *[He realises what he's saying]* ... Oh! Oops! Well, it's only a sort of *hobby* of mine ... *[MELANIE enters]*

SYLVIA *[warning him]*. Ahem!

'PATRICIA' *[getting the message]*. Sylvia, if you only knew how *glad* I am that there are no men working here. *[Accusingly]* They always pinch my bottom! *[SYLVIA fights to stay serious]*

MELANIE *[delighted, on her way through]*. Don't worry, Patricia, your bottom is safe in our hands – er ... I mean ... will be safe with us. And what a nice bottom it is! *['PATRICIA' seems undecided whether to appreciate the compliment]*

SYLVIA. Great! Now that's settled, Melanie, if you're going that way, can you find Rick O'Toole for me? He went off with Julia. We need to talk about something. Be a good sport. *[Persuasively]* I tell you what: I'll send Patricia over to you for a couple of days next week? You can give her some coaching in financial matters!

MELANIE. That's very noble of you, Sylvia. I'll see if I can find him. *[Throwing 'PATRICIA' another longing look]* I'm sure there's so much that I can teach Patricia. *[Exit]*

PATRICK *[breathing out]*. Bloody hell, I thought you were going to give me away!

SYLVIA. And miss out on some serious fun? Never!

PATRICK. But not at my expense! What did you mean, she could have me for a couple of days next week? I'm not a toy! Is she a lesbian? She was trying to get into my knickers!

SYLVIA. Melanie's sex life ... one of the great unsolved mysteries of the universe! We've got a sweepstake running on it! But seriously, though, Melanie's too confused to know what she wants. Probably something very spiritual and sisterly. And mystical. Oh, and vegetarian. Remember, 'Patricia' – you're a woman now. If you *really* want to know what we women have to put up with, your uncle Rick is on his way over. 'Mister Sex.' Let's see if *he* chats you up!

PATRICK. Oh, no! *[Pause]* This'll be a disaster. I should never have mentioned him! *[Starting to take off the disguise]* Let me get these things off. I don't want to work here.

SYLVIA. Patrick, stay a woman, *please*. For me? We can have some real fun with Melanie, especially if she *does* try to get into your knickers. And your uncle Rick has a *very* important role to play. Candida's already crazy about him.

PATRICK. So?

SYLVIA. So, just think about it – what will Candida do if 'Mister Sex' makes a play for someone else? *[He is horrified again]* Oh no, don't panic – I don't mean you! I mean someone *much* more interesting! You'll never guess! Hey, I'm so clever, sometimes I even scare myself.

[10]

Enter JULIA *and* RICK.

JULIA. Hallo, Sylvia. *[To* 'PATRICIA'*]* Hallo, you're Patricia, aren't you? This is Mr. O'Toole. Great guy. Great singer. Melanie asked me to bring him over. *[Ruefully touching her bottom]* If you have to take him anywhere, don't let him walk behind you. Got to go! *[Exit]*

RICK *[gazing after her]*. Pleasant girl, but too hectic. Still, you find the right little button to push, and she'll go off like a bomb!

SYLVIA. And you were searching for buttons …?

RICK. Look, Sylvia, *you* rang *me*. I got over here pretty fast. I'd like the job. I wouldn't say no to the money. So … where's the catch?

SYLVIA. I don't think you've met my new assistant yet, have you, Mr. O'Toole? This is Patricia. *[Now* RICK *notices* 'PATRICIA' *for the first time]* Patricia, this is 'Mister Sex.'

Pause. RICK *stares at* 'PATRICIA' *in complete amazement. He walks round 'her', looking at 'her' from different angles.*

RICK. So what's a lovely little cross-dresser like you doing in this part of town?

PATRICK *[to* SYLVIA*]*. See, it doesn't work, does it? Now let me get out of these things ...

RICK *[to* PATRICK*]*. No, it's really nice. It reminds me of you as a kid being forced to wear tights in winter. *[To* SYLVIA*]* Mothers shouldn't do that, the results are rather disturbing. *[To* PATRICK*]* All in all, I think you make quite a tasty woman, Patrick. Bit *rougher* than what I usually go for, perhaps ...

PATRICK *[indignantly]*. Now let's get this straight – this is a *political* thing, O.K.?

RICK *[unconvinced]*. Of course. *[Wistfully]* And the day started so well, me meeting Charlene and all. *[Pause. To* SYLVIA*]* Yes, Charlene! You didn't really think I was here just for the money, did you? Or to advertise your crappy products?

SYLVIA. But you haven't got the job yet. There is Jean-Pierre Lamour. They're doing a test film with Jean-Pierre and Charlene right now.

RICK *[with contempt]*. Jean-Pierre Lamour! The pseudo-Gallic slimebag! Mister Slobber-Kiss! It's enough to give the French a bad name!

SYLVIA. But he got there first. Candida is pushing him. He's made films with Charlene. He's the favourite! Although there is a way for you to get the contract. *[Pause] And* Charlene.

RICK. Great! Spill the beans!

SYLVIA. Bella has the last word. Make love to Bella, and the job is all yours!

RICK *[horrified]*. You must be mad! She'd eat me alive! That's not a woman, that's a tank of piranhas!

SYLVIA. I quite agree. *[Pause]* Look, just flirt with her. If *you* can't charm Bella, nobody can!

RICK. And what's in it for you? *[Looking from one to the other]* For *both* of you?

PATRICK. I want to show Cosfem. *[Scornfully]* 'Cosmetics *for* women *[Indicating himself]* by women'! I'm going to teach them a lesson! *[Hitching up his 'breasts']* And then I'll turn professional!

RICK *[laughing]*. And you, Sylvia?

SYLVIA. Bella has got to go. If we don't do it now, it'll be much harder later on.

RICK. And *how* precisely…? Don't forget – that is one carnivorous lady.

SYLVIA. If you flirt with Bella, and if you get the job, Candida won't like it … but that's just a personal thing between me and Candida. What's more important – Melanie won't like it either. And her family practically owns the company. She's already got one little surprise coming to her ...

PATRICK *[laughing, and readjusting his 'tits']*. I'm afraid so!

SYLVIA *[to* RICK*]*. And then you and Bella – shock number two! It'll be like the cat among the pigeons. A *tom cat*! With a bit of luck, we can bring down the tyrant! It might be the only way. Are you with me? *[Offering her hand]*

RICK *[pausing to think; then with a glint of mischief in his eye:]*. Just tell me what to do – I'm with you!

PATRICK. Me, too! Sorry! *[In a higher voice – concealing his Adam's apple with his hand]* Me, too! *[They all shake hands on the deal]*

Fade to black. Exeunt.

[video]

A banal advertisement for Cosfem lipstick starring CHARLENE.

CHARLENE *[oozingly]*.
            I am a woman.
  In the life of a woman ... *[Brandishing the lipstick]*
          there are events.
There are events in which a woman is most a woman.

There are events in which a woman is most herself.
For those *secret* events.
For the events that matter.
And because I am a woman.
For those events …
There is … *[Brandishing the lipstick again]*
Event.

<u>End of the first part of the play</u>

Part Two

[11]

The main office. Sitting in conference are: BELLA, BILL, CANDIDA, MELANIE, 'PATRICIA', SYLVIA *and, sitting slightly apart from them,* DESMOND *and* MISS CASKET *(who is taking notes).*

BELLA. Item one on the agenda of our meeting is – the name of our product. And I'm going to say it. I don't like 'Event'. We need something more powerful, more emotional.

BILL. Exactly – more *confrontational.*

MELANIE. We need a name that speaks to *women.*

BELLA. We need something more dramatic. It's strong. It's red. I suggest: 'Blood'.

BILL. You're not selling tampons.

BELLA. O.K. How about: 'Wound'?

CANDIDA. Why not: 'Cut'? *[With a slashing gesture of her hand across her lips]* 'The *cut* of love ...'

BELLA *[to* CANDIDA, *brutally].* Rubbish! But remind me to cut your *salary.* *[To* BILL*]* We need something imaginative, something that touches on deep fears and anxieties. What about: 'Vampire'?

BILL. Great, really upfront! But a touch too ... er ... Hollywood B-film?

BELLA. 'Mankiller'? It sends a powerful message, doesn't it?

MELANIE. But it's got 'man' in the name! Why not: 'Personkiller'? *[Everyone stares at her in disbelief]* No, no, alright ... Er ... 'Mercykiller'?

BELLA. Wait a moment. *[Pause]* 'Merciless'! 'She kills with her lips with Merciless!' Yes, I like that!

SYLVIA *[to herself]*. Woman red in tooth and claw ...

DESMOND *[delighted]*. You've been reading Tennyson!

CANDIDA *[to* BELLA, *who is not listening, however]*. Sylvia doesn't seem to approve. *[*SYLVIA *grimaces at* CANDIDA*]*

BELLA *[ignoring them both]*. 'Merciless' is a distinct possibility. Make a note of that. *[To* MISS CASKET*]* Who's taking notes – you *[Glancing at* DESMOND*]* or the new one?

MISS CASKET. *I'm* taking notes.

DESMOND *[jokingly to* MISS CASKET*]*. If you tell me

where to take them, I'll help you carry them! Sorry, just my little joke.

MISS CASKET *[putting a warning finger to her lips]*. Sshh!

DESMOND *[to* MISS CASKET*]*. Sorry! Nobody seems to have a sense of humour these days.

BELLA *[who fortunately hasn't heard him]*. Second item -

MELANIE *[interrupting]*. I would appreciate it very much if we could spend a few moments talking about the *feng-shui* in this office ...

CANDIDA. God, Melanie, you and your Chinese food, can't you eat normally like the rest of us?

MELANIE. Don't be so ignorant, Candida. I'm talking about things that *matter* – the influence of natural forces, of ... *[Looking around in a paranoid manner] force-fields*, on our physical and mental wellbeing!

BELLA. Force-fields are not on the agenda today.

MELANIE *[peevishly]*. Then I would like *feng-shui* to be *put* on the agenda for the next conference. And we can talk about astral influences as well. There are too many Scorpios here, it's very difficult to work properly.

SYLVIA. What have you got against Scorpios?

CANDIDA *[to* MELANIE*]. You're* obviously a Virgo!

SYLVIA. Well, you obviously *aren't*, Candida!

MELANIE *[to* 'PATRICIA'*]*. You aren't a Scorpio, are you Patricia?

BELLA. If we've got too many Scorpios, then get rid of some of them. We have to cut costs around here ...

MELANIE. These things are important. *You* know what I'm talking about, don't you, Patricia?

'PATRICIA' *[confused]*. Um, right ... I'm sure we'd all be much better off if we watched our *feng-shui* now and then. *[*MELANIE *is delighted and gives him/her a big smile]*

BELLA *[irritated]*. I think we'll take a break here. *[Looking around impatiently]* Where's that wretched P-R woman? *[To* CANDIDA*]* You do it, then – I need some of those stupid advertising labels, you know, the little one-inch cardboard lips for sticking on Christmas and birthday presents, just a couple of hundred to start with. See that it gets done. *[Getting up]* Alright – half an hour, ladies, that should be enough.

Exeunt BELLA, BILL, MELANIE, 'PATRICIA' *and* SYLVIA.

CANDIDA [*to* MISS CASKET]. You can type that, can't you?

MISS CASKET. No, I have to collect the post. But Mr. Barrow here will help you, won't you Desmond? [*Exit*]

CANDIDA. Bloody woman! [*To* DESMOND] Well, *you* can write it for me, then. You *can* write, can't you?

DESMOND [*beaming*]. I'm a writer!

CANDIDA [*gesturing at the word-processor*]. Then switch it on, and I'll be back in just a mo. Be careful with the mouse, though, you need to twiddle it a bit. And check the emails too. [*Exit*]

[12]

DESMOND *confronts the computer.*

DESMOND. Since I'm sitting at the computer anyway, I might as well write the first chapter of my novel. Inspiration struck me with the perfect beginning. [*Looking at the screen*] What's this rubbish? 'Enter password to unlock screen saver'? Dear oh me, somebody could have *told* me the password ... [*Pause*] What could it be? [*Pause*] Well, they're all women here. What is it that women think about all the time? [*Pause*] Let's try that ... [*He types a word*] Aha, there you go!! Desmond, did you know that you were a genius? *[Pause as the programme loads.* DESMOND *flexes his fingers over the keyboard like a concert pianist]* Alright, muse, give me your best. *[Reading to himself as he is typing]* 'It was a dark and stormy night ...' Yes, I like that!

Enter CANDIDA, *who looks at* DESMOND *in amazement.*

CANDIDA. What do you think you're doing?

DESMOND *[feeling guilty and caught]*. Just doing what you told me to. *[Trying to change the subject]* Oh, by the way, you were right about the mouse, it doesn't work all too well. In fact, it reminds me of that poem by Robert Burns, the Scottish dialect poet, you know, the one about a little mouse. I can't do a proper Scottish accent of course!: 'Wee, sleekit, cow'rin', tim'rous beastie, O what a panic's in thy breastie!' It makes you feel quite sorry for mice, doesn't it?

CANDIDA *[very puzzled]*. Er, yes ... who told you the password, anyway?

DESMOND. Why, nobody. I figured that out on my own.

CANDIDA. What!?

DESMOND. That's the advantage of being a writer, isn't it? It was simple, really. What do you need to know to understand feminine nature? I just pretended to be a woman and the word sprang to my mind immediately!

CANDIDA *[To herself]*. Oh great, now they're really on to us! *[To* DESMOND*]* Since you're so clever, I've got a little job for you. It's something very easy, you can phone it through to them and write the letter afterwards. We want to order some lips, right? From our usual supplier, they're just down the street from here, that Casket woman will give you their details. The usual sort, cardboard, er, two hundred, er, inch-size lips. Alright?

DESMOND. Yes, I've got that. But how many?

CANDIDA. Two hundred – I've just told you! Good gracious, you *are* slow on the uptake!

DESMOND. Not at all. Actually …

CANDIDA *[quickly]*. Don't start that 'actually' nonsense again! *[With an imperious gesture]* Go! Your mistress commands! *[Tapping her wristwatch]* Speed is of the essence! There's a good boy!

DESMOND *[muttering]*. Do this! Do that! I should be working on my book … *[Exit, as* RICK *enters]*

CANDIDA *[shaking her head in disbelief]*. Weird, weird …

[13]

RICK *[looking in the direction in which* DESMOND *exited]*. Bad vibrations?

CANDIDA *[intense]*. I see you are a man who is very sensitive to vibrations. Especially when a *woman* is around.

RICK *[suspecting something]*. Perhaps ... *[Pause]* By the way, should we be talking to each other? Aren't I the enemy, or something?

CANDIDA *[heavy]*. I want Jean-Pierre for this campaign. He'd be better. *[Pause]* But I would take *you* for *everything else*, any day! *[She steps forward, and* RICK *steps back]*

RICK. That's very flattering.

CANDIDA. No. Not flattering. I say what I think. I know what I want – and I usually get it.

RICK. This is an interesting situation. Cool. Very much so.

CANDIDA. Rick, let's not waste time! You and I, we could be *big* – Romeo and Juliet, Antony and Cleopatra.

RICK. Those were tragedies. Didn't they all die?

CANDIDA *[ignoring this]*. I've waited a lifetime for this moment. When you walked in, my whole body went ... *[Shuddering ecstatically]* aaawh! That is a call that, when it comes, every woman must answer. Rick ... give me that call. Just take me ... here ... now ... on this table! *[As she lunges towards him, he steps back]*

RICK. You like forceful men?

CANDIDA. I like my men to be *big* – big ambitions, big actions, big gestures, big *[With a sigh]* in *every* way! I like them *big*!

RICK. Me too.

There is a complete change of mood, like the temperature dropping suddenly. Pause. **CANDIDA** *steps back, very surprised.*

CANDIDA. What do you mean? Are you gay or something? God, what a nightmare!

RICK. No, I'm not gay. Candida, you like strong men. Well, I like strong, powerful women.

CANDIDA. That's settled then – no problem *there*!

RICK. Yes, there is.

CANDIDA. No, there isn't.

RICK. Candida, there is someone else. Someone who ... makes my heart sing.

CANDIDA *[sarcastically]*. Who makes everything groovy, right? Who is this creep? I'll soon sort *her* out! Who is it? It's not Sylvia, surely?

RICK. No, it's Bella, your boss.

CANDIDA *[stunned]*. Oh. *[Pause. Then, recovering]* And you think she's more attractive than I am? I can't believe that!

RICK. But you have to.

CANDIDA. But can't you see what I'm offering you? I am a woman ...

RICK. I think I know that text! *[Necessarily brutal]* Look, Candida, let's be honest – you're not really my type. You know, even if they tied you to me naked, and there was an earthquake, force seven-and-a-half on the Richter Scale, nothing would move. Not even my small toenail. *[Nastily]* That's the way life is, darling!

CANDIDA *[outraged]*. You bastard!

RICK *[coolly]*. Let's try to keep this professional? *[Provocatively]* By the way, my rehearsal with Charlene was good. That girl digs me too. I think I'm going to be the new lipstick man! Must be going – see you later *[As* BILL *enters]* and look, here's your consolation prize, young Mr. Bullshit! *[Exit]*

BILL *[staring at* RICK*'s retreating back]*. I don't like that man one little bit. But I don't think that Jean-Pierre is in any danger. He's got *real* class, *real* sex appeal.

CANDIDA *[dazed, and still very hurt]*. What do you know about things like that? You haven't got a clue!

BILL. Hey hey hey! Hold your horses! This is Bill Bullock you're talking to. From BAM. When I was at college, they called me 'King of the Campus'. I hit those first-year girls like a rocket. *And* the au pair girls. *And* those little Swedish language students. I reckon the British condom industry should've given me a medal.

CANDIDA *[indignant]*. You are unbelievable!

BILL *[getting into chatting-up mood]*. Yes, I know. And the good news is: I'm currently available. Don't spread it around, though, or I'll have to take my telephone off the hook, haha. *[Leering]* But I can fit you in, tonight even. I know a cosy, candle-lit bistro, not far from my flat. They have a table in a quiet corner that is permanently reserved for Bill Bullock. There is a …

CANDIDA *[exploding]*. Did you know that you are the most unmitigated, godforsaken little turd that I have ever met? I have trodden in dog's excrement with more sex appeal than you have! I doubt if you could give pleasure to a fruit salad, let alone a woman! *[Looking in the direction in which* RICK *left]* That guy may be a total bastard, he may be a heartbreaker, but at least he's a man! *[Turning towards* BILL *again]* Mr. Bullock, give me Jean-Pierre Lamour, help me get that TV spot for him, but otherwise: keep your dirty hands and your dirty thoughts to yourself. O.K.? *[Exit]*

BILL *[unfazed but uncomprehending]*. What is wrong with all these women? There is something about the atmosphere around here ... *[Throwing up his hands]* They're all lesbians! But I won't give up. And tonight, one of these women is going to have an unforgettable, life-changing experience. With Bill Bullock.

[14]

Enter SYLVIA *and* 'PATRICIA'. 'PATRICIA' *is now wearing a scarf round her neck.*

BILL *[relieved]*. Wow! You lovely ladies are a sight for sore eyes. Just what the doctor ordered ...

SYLVIA *[puzzled]*. Pardon?

'PATRICIA' *[ditto]*. Come again?

BILL. I have just had the most depressing conversation with your colleague Candida. Something about her isn't quite right. Maybe it's her hormones? *You* ladies don't have that problem, do you? I got an instinct for that sort of thing! *[Change of tone]* Look, I have a great idea. What say we get together over a drink sometime? Tonight even? I know a lovely little restaurant. Candle-lit. Not far from here.

SYLVIA *[pretending to be shocked]*. Both of us, Mr. Bullock?

BILL *[preeningly]*. Why not? One man, two women. Women who are tolerant, with a modern attitude to life. A man who is capable of, er, rising to the challenge. Of course, if you prefer, I'm sure I can find two separate evenings. They have a table permanently reserved for me. In a quiet corner.

SYLVIA. No chance, I'm afraid. Sorry. I'm having my hair done. Always takes hours!

BILL *[to* 'PATRICIA'*]*. That just leaves you and me, sweetheart.

'PATRICIA' *[panicky]*. I'm having my hair done, too! Takes even longer.

BILL. And tomorrow?

'PATRICIA'. Er ... I'm buying a new dress! Takes ages and ages.

BILL. And the day after?

'PATRICIA'. I'll be going on vacation. Honolulu.

BILL. I thought you only started here today ... *[Suddenly suspicious]* Or have you got something against me? Don't say *you're* lesbians too? Like Candida?

SYLVIA. *Candida a lesbian? [Pause]* Look, Bill, you're a very attractive man ...

BILL. I know.

SYLVIA. ... but it wouldn't be fair.

BILL. It wouldn't be fair?

SYLVIA. And do you know why? Because there's someone who *really* likes you, but she's too shy to tell you. Anyway, Patsy here and I wouldn't be right for you. We're not lesbians ...

'PATRICIA' *[outraged]*. Most certainly not!

SYLVIA. ... but we're very much into each other *emotionally.* Aren't we, my honeybun?

'PATRICIA' *[not happy]*. Are we?

SYLVIA. Of course. *[To* BILL*]* Women are a bit like that. You're an experienced man, you know about that sort of thing, don't you?

BILL *[clueless]*. Er, yeah, of course.

SYLVIA. You're *so* understanding …

BILL *[changing tack]*. Yeah, well, who's this other chick, then, the one who fancies me?

Enter MELANIE.

SYLVIA. Hallo, Melanie.

MELANIE *[to* BILL*]*. Have you seen Bella? *[Behind her back,* SYLVIA *gestures to* BILL *that 'This is the one!']* I've just had a call from our paper suppliers. Someone has sent them a *very* strange order. A man, they said. Seems very unlikely to me. They're already making the things, though, and they're sending them over. [Tenderly] Hallo Patricia.

SYLVIA *[seizing* 'PATRICIA'*'s hand]*. Patsy, you and I aren't needed – here are two people who want to be alone. *[To* BILL*]* Mr. Bullock …

BILL. Call me Bill!

SYLVIA *[to* BILL*]*. All right, Bill, remember what I told you, and act accordingly! Come on, Patsy, dear, we've got a company to save. *[Exeunt* SYLVIA *and* 'PATRICIA'*]*

BILL. That girl is *so* bright. Absolutely on the ball! Tip-top!

MELANIE. On the contrary, I didn't understand a single word she was saying. But her behaviour with Patricia is tasteless in the extreme.

BILL. Come on, everybody knows what women do when they're among themselves.

MELANIE. No. What?

BILL *[the wind taken out of his sails]*. You know ... *[Getting on with the programme]* Well, anyway, so you're a bit shy. That's no problem, I like it that way. It's really very simple. *[Puffing himself up]* Me: man. You: woman. Let your body speak!

MELANIE. I beg your pardon?

BILL. O.K., you never done it – I can dig that.

MELANIE. Never done *what*?

BILL. But I can see the truth in your eyes. There's something very special about your eyes. They're like *[Struggling]* ... er ... a rice pudding!

MELANIE. What, cold and sticky and fattening?

BILL. No, delicious to eat! Look, don't spoil this moment! Because you're making *me* happy too. I knew that this was a big lezzie setup when I came here. That Bella. And Candida. And those two. But no problem, I can live with that.

MELANIE. I think there is a misunderstanding here, Mr. Bullock.

BILL. Call me Bill! *Billy... [Leering]* But I'll tell you something. There's no such thing as a lesbian, right? What there is, baby, is a woman who's never been *serviced* properly. Know what I mean? Like the vegetarian who's never had a good steak. But *you* like meat, don't you?

MELANIE. No, not at all!

BILL. O.K., you're a woman who gets straight to the point. I like that! We cut the food and go to my place for drinkies by candle-light. I've got some great sounds, Barry White, Barry Manilow, Julio Iglesias, all the classics. And then – we take off for paradise! *[Seizing her hand and placing it on his biceps]* Feel that: Solid muscle, five years in the gym!

MELANIE. Help!! *[JULIA enters, and MELANIE throws herself into her arms]*

JULIA. Really, Mr. Bullock, is this your idea of 'active marketing'?

BILL *[throwing up his hands in frustration]*. How can a woman be normal in a place like this? *[*JULIA's *mobile phone goes off with a ridiculous signal]*

JULIA. Johnson! Julia! P-R! *[Pause]* Yes! *[Pause]* No. *[Pause]* Yes, she's here, but she's just been half-raped. *[Pause]* Just a joke. *[Pause]* See you later, then. But let me talk to Melanie first. O.K. *Adios. [To* BILL, *as* JEAN-PIERRE, RICK *and* CHARLENE *enter]* Naughty, naughty Mr. Bullock! *[Wagging her finger]* Bad boy! *[Exeunt* JULIA *and* MELANIE*]*

RICK *[grinning, and copying* JULIA's *gesture]*. Naughty, naughty …

BILL *[furious]*. You're in for a kidney punch, mate! *[To* JEAN-PIERRE*]* I'll see you later, Jean-Pierre. And I wouldn't get too close to *him* if I were you, you'll probably catch something. They've all had too much beef – the whole place is full of mad cows. *[Exit]*

[15]

CHARLENE. Rude young fellow, that student. Needs a good smacked bottom.

JEAN-PIERRE. 'E is a good boy, *chérie*. But 'is generation … a 'ole generation without manners. *[Stiffly]* You can't learn manners from video games. *[To* RICK*] N'est-ce pas*, Rick?

RICK. How's your back, soldier?

JEAN-PIERRE *[starting]*. Oh, please don't touch! It will be better soon. A massage, a cup of tea ...

CHARLENE. I'm sorry it didn't go so well this time, Jean-Pierre. Maybe I should do this one with Rick. It's only a silly lipstick ad.

JEAN-PIERRE *[with great dignity]*. I shall save myself for our next film together, *ma chère*.

RICK. No hard feelings, old man, O.K.? I bet you and Charlene have got some fantastic projects lined up!

JEAN-PIERRE *[spaciously]*. There are plans for an epic film, a masterpiece about the fall of the Roman Empire: *Nero – The Glory and the Passion*. I play the tragic *empereur* who gives up everything for the Christian slave-girl, played by *[Turning stiffly to point to her]* Charlene. There is a wonderful orgy scene with *naked* slave-girls. Charlene is also ... *naked*.

CHARLENE. Oh, good!

JEAN-PIERRE. They make long, passionate love. Many times! It will be a beautiful film. Sensitive and tasteless *[Correcting himself]* er, *tasteful*. It will be our greatest achievement! *[Nobly]* Take her, Rick, for this advertisement she is yours! I shall rest, and then prepare myself for the ordeal of the film studio. *[Self-importantly]* Also, I 'ave a secret ... a secret of the 'eart.

RICK. Hey, there's some bird you fancy, right?

JEAN-PIERRE. Ah, the British, so down-to-earth, so ... *unromantic*. *[Pause]* Yes, Rick, you could phrase it like that, if you must.

CHARLENE *[pretending to be annoyed]*. Jean-Pierre, don't say that you've been disloyal to me!

JEAN-PIERRE. *Chérie*, our love is for the centuries. For eternity. A thousand years from now they will watch our films and they will think ... *sacrebleu, that was love!* *[Change of tone]* 'Owever, I need someone to massage my back, and make my tea, and *[Smiling]* warm my 'eart – and I 'ave found such a woman!

RICK. Good for you! *[CHARLENE gives JEAN-PIERRE an affectionate kiss]* Who is it, then?

JEAN-PIERRE. When the time comes, you will find out.

RICK. I've found a bird, too, and she's fantastic – but for the moment I can't tell you more than that.

CHARLENE. Good heavens, I've never heard so many mysteries before! I'm not surprised, though – when it comes to romance, men don't know what's going on. *[Looking at them]* Stop looking like sheep, you two! I know the male psyche, and whatever it is you're burbling about, romance ain't part of it. You've got your couple of little tricks, I grant you that, but it's all so predictable. Sometimes I think: Why bother? I might just as well go home and do some ironing or something.

JEAN-PIERRE. Is this the Charlene with whom I 'ave shared so many moments of tenderness?

CHARLENE. I'm afraid it is, Jean-Pierre. And *I'm* not getting any younger either. I'm going for a lie-down. *[Exit]*

RICK. She's right, isn't she?

JEAN-PIERRE *[shocked]*. You too, Rick? Is there no more romance in the world?

RICK. Let's be honest, Jean-Pierre – 'Mr. Sex', 'The Man Whose Name is Love', and all that stuff. Wouldn't you rather have a quiet night in, with a nice film on the telly (one of yours and Charlene's, even, though I hate to say it!), some good home cooking, a warm, comfy bed with an electric blanket?

JEAN-PIERRE. A nice cuppa tea. Some chocolate biscuits. Someone to massage my back. Aah!

RICK. It's not our world any more. It belongs to the young ...

Exeunt. Fade to black.

[video]

Another take for 'Young Event', but this time with two actors and much slicker.

FEMALE 'YOUNG EVENT' *[very feminine].*
      Hey, cool, when he looks at me
          I wanna know

MALE 'YOUNG EVENT' *[macho].*
      At moments like this
      I lose all control.

FEMALE 'YOUNG EVENT'.
      Me and my lipstick
      Are goin' somewhere

MALE 'YOUNG EVENT'.
          Hey baby!

FEMALE 'YOUNG EVENT'.
      And the rest of the world
      Had better take care!

MALE 'YOUNG EVENT'.
      You goin' somewhere?
      Wanna go with *me*?

FEMALE 'YOUNG EVENT'.
Young Event [Brandishing a phallic-looking lipstick
      at the camera]

MALE 'YOUNG EVENT'.
What every man wants, baby.
Just wait and see!

FEMALE 'YOUNG EVENT'.
Young Event [Waving the lipstick again] – oh yeah!

JOANNA *[off-camera].* And cut!

[16]

The lights come up to reveal BELLA, BILL, CANDIDA, JEAN-PIERRE, MELANIE, 'PATRICIA', SYLVIA *and (sitting slightly apart from them)* DESMOND *and* MISS CASKET. *They have just been watching the 'Young Event' advertisement.* MELANIE *glares at* BILL *occasionally.* CANDIDA *is sulking.*

BELLA. God, young people, don't they make you sick?! Still, we need this market. And that was a *much* more professional effort.

SYLVIA. They were professional actors.

MELANIE. *She* was particularly appealing.

BELLA. *He* looks stupid, but he's cute. Get him into tighter pants. I want everything to show.

MELANIE *[shocked].* Bella, really!

BELLA. Come on, we're in this to make money, aren't we? The camera pans from the lipstick she's holding down to what he's got in his pants. This is 'Young Event'. This is what it does to men – *that's* the message we want to send.

MELANIE [*starting to rant*]. *That's* the message you want to send? Shouldn't we rise above such primitive genital fixation? The future belongs to *us*. Men are irrelevant. We don't need to mention them so often. And we should try to avoid the word 'woman', too. It's humiliating, building *our* name out of *theirs*!

SYLVIA. Surely the word 'woman', by containing the word 'man', incorporates it? So 'woman' is greater than 'man'!

DESMOND. 'Woman' was originally something like 'wife-man' in Anglo-Saxon, if that's of any help.

BELLA. O.K., O.K., can we get back to business? Although Melanie is essentially right ...

SYLVIA. So you're saying – don't use *either* word, 'man' *or* 'woman'?

MISS CASKET. I would have to change all the correspondence.

BELLA [*unleashing her anger on an easy target*]. If you feel that your talents are being wasted on us, Miss Birdbrain, then take them elsewhere. Otherwise, do the work that you're paid for!

JEAN-PIERRE *[indignantly]*. I must protest! This is *abominable*! I cannot work with people who 'ave so little respect for … for …

BELLA. Who *says* that you're going to be working for us, Monsieur Lamour? *That* will be decided by the next couple of minutes and by the *effort* – and 'effort' is probably the right word in this case – that you and Charlene produced a little earlier today. Perhaps we should view this masterpiece?

The lights are dimmed.

[video]

Scene with CHARLENE *and* JEAN-PIERRE.

CHARLENE *[oozingly]*.
        I am a woman.

JEAN-PIERRE *[dripping with Gallic charm]*.
        I am *ze man.*

JOANNA *[off-camera]*. No, it's '*a* man'. Look at the text, Jean-Pierre.

JEAN-PIERRE *[defensively]*. But that is not logical. There is only *one* man in 'er life. It is *me*.

JOANNA *[off-camera]*. No, I'm sure about this. Look at your text for a moment.

CHARLENE. Jean-Pierre, I think you will find that Joanna is right on this one.

JOANNA *[off-camera]*. Can we do this again, please? We'll cut, and do a retake.

The same scene again.

CHARLENE *[oozingly]*.
          I am a woman.

JEAN-PIERRE *[ditto]*.
          I am *a man*.

CHARLENE.
    In the life of a woman ... there are events.
There are events in which a woman is most a woman.
  There are events in which a woman is most herself.

JEAN-PIERRE.
      In the life of a woman ... there is
[They move towards each other to kiss, but CHARLENE *blunders short-sightedly past him]* – a man? Charlene?

CHARLENE. Where are you then?

JEAN-PIERRE *[distraught]*. Charlene!

JOANNA *[off-camera]*. Cut!!

The same scene for a third time.

JEAN-PIERRE.
    In the life of a woman ... there is
[They move towards each other to kiss, but JEAN-PIERRE *pulls up suddenly]* – oh my back!.

CHARLENE. Oh my darling, what's happened?

JOANNA *[off-camera]*. Hallo, for some reason we seem to have left the script. I do suggest that we keep to the script, please! Are you quite alright, Monsieur Lamour? Cut.

The same scene for a fourth time. CHARLENE *and* JEAN-PIERRE *get through to the end this time, but* JEAN-PIERRE *clutches grotesquely at his back throughout the take.*

CHARLENE *[oozingly]*.
    I am a woman.

JEAN-PIERRE *[ditto]*.
    I am *a man*.

CHARLENE.
    In the life of a woman ... there are events.
There are events in which a woman is most a woman.
There are events in which a woman is most herself.

JEAN-PIERRE.
>In the life of a woman ... there is a man.

CHARLENE.
>For the man who matters
>And because I am a woman
>For those events ... and for that man
>There is ... *[Brandishing the lipstick]*
>Event.

Fade to black.

[17]

The lights come up to reveal BELLA, BILL, CANDIDA, JEAN-PIERRE, MELANIE, 'PATRICIA', SYLVIA *and, sitting slightly apart from them,* DESMOND *and* MISS CASKET.

BELLA. Awful, awful. In fact, it beggars belief. But maybe we could sell it to the BBC as a new comedy series. Jean-Pierre battling with the English language. Jean-Pierre struggling with the problem of taking two steps across a room. And then comes the big question: Can Charlene see him at all? It's like *The Night of the Living Dead*! There'a a wonderful new storyline every week!

MISS CASKET *[to* DESMOND*]*. How do you spell 'awful', with or without an 'e'?

DESMOND. Without an 'e'.

MISS CASKET. Thank you so much, Mr. Barrow... er, Desmond.

DESMOND. We writers have to know that sort of thing.

BELLA *[to* JEAN-PIERRE, *who is looking hangdog].* Let me make myself clear. We can't possibly take you, Monsieur Lamour, so ... why don't you just go back to Manchester? You can settle your expenses with Melanie before you leave. It will have to be Rick O'Toole after all – 'Mister Sex'!

MISS CASKET. How can you be so heartless? How can you be so rude to such a wonderful man?

JEAN-PIERRE *[looking up].* Lavinia!

MISS CASKET. Someone has to say it – she's a nasty woman.

CANDIDA *[quietly].* And *I* know why she's so keen on Rick O'Toole ...

BELLA *[glaring at* MISS CASKET*].* What is this – Mutiny on the Bounty?

BILL *[self-importantly].* I think it's time for BAM to make a statement. *[Clearing his throat]* Holding as we do the exclusive rights to Mr. Jean-Pierre Lamour in connection with …

JEAN-PIERRE *[with a dismissive wave]*. Forget it, Bill, I'm going back to Manchester.

BILL. No, hold on, mate! *[To* BELLA*]* My client was seriously let down by the unexpectedly weak performance of his partner.

BELLA *[thoughtfully]*. So: *he* was crap because *Charlene* was crap. It's possible, I suppose. Well, there's only one way to find out. Try him out with another partner. Which of you ladies would like to have a go?

MELANIE. Surely Patricia would be the best choice? She's the youngest, and so unmistakably feminine.

'PATRICIA' *[terrified]*. Oh no, I don't think so.

SYLVIA. Come on, no false modesty, Patsy!

BILL *[pulling out some papers]*. And it just so happens that I've produced a little something for 'Event', based on Bella's fantastic idea for a new name. There you go!

JEAN-PIERRE *[reading half-heartedly]*.
    One bite and it was love.

'PATRICIA'.
    I am a woman.

JEAN-PIERRE.
>She killed me with 'er eyes.

'PATRICIA'.
>Bam, bam!

BELLA *[interrupting]*. Bam, bam? What rubbish is this?

BILL *[explaining]*. This is the sexual encounter seen as a gunfight. A shootout.

CANDIDA. It's pathetic.

BILL. It's meant to be symbolic.

CANDIDA. Of what? Your chat-up technique?

SYLVIA. Bam, bam! Let me guess – free advertising for your agency?

BELLA. We might as well hear the rest, I suppose.

JEAN-PIERRE *[reading again]*.
>She killed me with 'er lips.

'PATRICIA'.
>I killed him with my lips!

JEAN-PIERRE.
>With *Merciless*!

'PATRICIA'.
I killed him with *Merciless* …

BILL *[enthusiastic]*. And then they kiss. *[Looking at* JEAN-PIERRE *and* 'PATRICIA' *expectantly]* And what we need here is a really powerful, full-contact kiss. They've got to slam into each other, really *chew* at each other. *[Pause]* O.K.? *[Pause]* Well, go on!

'PATRICIA' *[horrified]*. Oh… yes… well… no… oh dear…

JEAN-PIERRE. No.

BELLA *[angry]*. What do you mean – no?

JEAN-PIERRE *[Olympian]*. Jean-Pierre is not in ze mood.

BILL *[amazed]*. But you're the big kisser!

'PATRICIA'. I'm not in the mood either!

MELANIE *[rushing to her side]*. Oh, poor Patricia!

JEAN-PIERRE. This girl is too … immature. With Charlene – anytime. But I 'ave been deeply wounded in my professional pride. And *[Indicating* MISS CASKET*]* this wonderful *mademoiselle* 'as been gravely insulted. *[Tenderly]* Lavinia …

MISS CASKET. Thank you, Jean-Pierre. *[To* BELLA*]*

I'm not a birdbrain!

DESMOND. Hear, hear!

MISS CASKET. But *you're* a bad person, Arabella Merchant, and it's about time that somebody told you that!

BELLA. So I'm a bad person, am I? Well, at least this bad person has got a job, unlike other people I know. Pack your stuff, birdbrain, you're fired.

MISS CASKET. You can't do that! I've been in this company for ...

BELLA. ... far too long already. You heard me. Begone!

MISS CASKET. Oh, is that so? Well, you can't fire me! Because I quit! So there!

BELLA. Suits me. In that case we'll even save the redundancy money. *[Pause]* You still here?

MISS CASKET. No, I wouldn't spend another second in your presence. *[About to leave]*

JEAN-PIERRE. And I am goin' too. Perhaps you will allow me to accompany you, *ma chérie*?

MISS CASKET. I would be deeply honoured, Jean-Pierre. You come back to my place and I'll make you a nice cup of tea –

JEAN-PIERRE. *Sacrebleu*! A temptation that I cannot resist!

MISS CASKET. – and I'll give your poor old back a massage, too.

DESMOND. What a noble gesture. *[Exeunt* JEAN-PIERRE *and* MISS CASKET*]*

BELLA. Now, are there any more smart remarks? No, I didn't think there would be. *[*JULIA *enters carrying a huge pair of lips]* If I asked you what that is, would I like the answer?

JULIA. Something that we ordered, apparently. *[She puts the lips down]* But *I* have work to do. *[Exit]*

BELLA *[chasing after* JULIA*]*. Julia! Come back here at once! *[Running into* RICK *as he enters]* Oh, it's you. Perhaps you've come at the right moment. You can read in for Jean-Pierre. We'll do the spot with you and Charlene. Sorry, Mr. Bullock, but your client has gone. Perhaps you can learn to work with Mr. O'Toole?

RICK. We've.. um ... had our differences, Mr. Bullock ...

BILL *[grabbing* RICK*'s hand]*. Welcome on board, Rick! 'Mr. Sex'! That's an image that BAM can do things with. We're moving away from sophisticated Latin Lover, and into new territory: Action Man! *[To* BELLA*]* Hey, what say we try him out with Patricia first? There's a market out there waiting to be tapped. All those young girls who are crazy about older men. All those secretaries who fancy the boss.

BELLA *[as* 'PATRICIA' *panics]*. That's a great idea.

MELANIE *[supportively]*. I don't think this is right for our company. I don't think Patricia wants to go through with this.

CANDIDA. I agree with Melanie. They wouldn't look right as a couple.

BELLA. Nonsense. Just do it.

SYLVIA. Bella, there's something that Mr. O'Toole wants to talk to you about. In private. *[Giving* RICK *a heavy look]* That's right, isn't it, Mr. O'Toole?

RICK. Oh, yes, quite right!

BELLA. Then 'Mr. Sex' and I will have a little talk. The rest of you can go powder your noses for five minutes. But be back here on time. Time is money! And I want no more criticism from any of you lot – *or else. [She makes a cut-throat gesture. Exeunt everybody except* BELLA *and* RICK*]*

[18]

BELLA. So *you* don't want to do this advert, either?

RICK. No, it's not as easy as that. *[Pause]* I don't want to do it with Patricia, though, she's too young, she's not professional.

BELLA. Well, Charlene, then.

RICK. Alright. It wouldn't mean anything to *her*. Or to me. It would be just a job. *[Intensely]* But I would be thinking about someone else as I kissed her.

BELLA *[scornfully]*. Don't most men?

RICK *[seductively]*. Bella, there's something about you. You have a strength unlike any other woman I've ever met. You have an... aura that is magnetic.

BELLA *[surprised]*. Oh!

RICK. You know, most men feel intimidated when they face a strong, charismatic woman, a woman who is a natural leader. But I don't, I feel inspired. *[Turning away dramatically]* Ah, I've revealed too much about myself!

BELLA *[warming]*. Oh, not at all, Rick. I may call you Rick?

RICK. I would be *so* honoured. But tell me, Bella –

what made you the extraordinary person that you are?

BELLA. You'll never guess, Rick. I was the youngest of six children. *[Then grimly]* And all the others were boys! *[Pause. Then furiously]* It was: 'Bella do this!' 'Bella do that!' Who had to do the dishes? Bella! Who had to clean Grandma's bathroom? Bella, of course! Bella had to do everything! And who got that extra piece of meat? It wasn't Bella! Well – *never again*!

RICK *[pretending to be impressed]*. But it brought you to where you are today, Bella! The very top! You're so strong, I'm frightened of you!

BELLA. Maybe I misjudged you, Rick, you're actually a sensible kind of guy. *[Pause]* It would make me very happy if you could do the ad.

RICK. Bella, I'll do it for you! With Charlene, not Patricia of course. But it'll be *you* I'll be thinking of …

BELLA. Good, that's settled. I'll call them back in. *[Exit.* RICK *sinks his head onto his hands.* SYLVIA, CANDIDA, JULIA, MELANIE, 'PATRICIA', BILL *and* DESMOND *reenter]*

[19]

SYLVIA *[to* RICK*]*. Still alive? She didn't bite anything off?

CANDIDA. Judas!

JULIA. Give the guy a break, he survived, didn't he? *[BELLA reenters, primping her hair rather vainly]*

BELLA. Gather round, everyone! *[Noticing* JULIA*]* Hey, what an honour to have *Julia* among us once again! But don't let us keep you from more important matters! Are you sure that you don't have a cellphone or a camera to play with? Or something that needs to be *carried*?

JULIA. No, Joanna's doing that for a while. *[Enter* JOANNA, *who is carrying another set of lips]*

JOANNA. Hi, folks, here's another one! *[She puts the lips down and exits]*

BELLA *[fuming]*. And what is that? *[To* CANDIDA*]* Candida, is this another one of *your* little tricks? Some sort of joke, perhaps? Well, it comes at just the right moment to give me a good excuse, sorry, a good *reason* to terminate your contract with this company.

CANDIDA. *I* didn't order the silly thing!

DESMOND. Actually, I'm afraid you did.

CANDIDA. No I didn't.

DESMOND. Yes you did. You gave me the order.

CANDIDA. I ordered two hundred inch-size lips.

DESMOND. Correct. And that's exactly what I ordered: Two-hundred-inch-size lips. You see: *[Pointing]* Lips. *[Gesture of measuring]* Two hundred inches.

BELLA *[to* DESMOND*]*. You stupid man, you passed on the wrong order!

DESMOND. That is what happens when people fail to express themselves in clear, grammatical English. And there is no need to be abusive. It's unnecessary, and you don't seem to realise how *hurtful* it can be.

CANDIDA. So – instead of ordering two hundred *little* sets of lips, you ordered *[Counting them with her finger]* two *big* ones?

DESMOND. Who said anything about *two* big ones?

Enter JOANNA, *carrying a third pair of giant lips.*

JOANNA. Shall I put this with the other ones?

JULIA. Yes, make a little pile. And the rest of them, too.

BELLA. The rest of them?!

Exit JOANNA. *Enter* CHARLENE, *carrying two more sets of giant lips.*

CHARLENE. Where do these go, Julia? *[Peering myopically]* Julia, where are you?

JULIA. I'm over here!

CHARLENE *blunders towards her, charges into* BELLA *with her giant lips, swings one way and hits* CANDIDA, *swings the other and hits* MELANIE: *There is total chaos.*

CHARLENE. I don't mind helping a bit, but I can't carry them *all* – there must be dozens of them!

BELLA. Dozens?!!

DESMOND. Again, this inexact use of language. No wonder that the wrong things get ordered. You asked for two hundred, so by my calculation there must be another one hundred and ninety-five of the things. Although I can't quite see what they're useful for.

JULIA. Hey, no! This is great P.R. stuff. We can do *such a lot* with giant lips.

BELLA. Like what?

JULIA. Hmm, ha … good question! Now try me with another one – but a bit easier this time, please! Hey, I know someone who can help us! *[She starts punching a number on her mobile phone]*

BELLA *[furious]*. Switch that bloody thing off! Now,

gather round – Rick and I have got something we want to announce.

RICK *[surprised]*. Have we?

BELLA *[warmly]*. Of course, my dear. *[To the whole group]* Rick has agreed to do the 'Merciless' spot for us. *[To* CHARLENE*]* With Charlene. *[To* RICK*]* Come here, sweetheart! Come on, hop hop!

CANDIDA *[whispering]*. What a disgusting spectacle – he's sold himself to her!

SYLVIA *[to* CANDIDA*]*. Just because your candidate didn't win?

MELANIE. No, Candida is right. Look at the way she is sucking up to him!

BELLA. What are you on about, Melanie? Muttering like an old woman!

MELANIE. But at least I *am* still a woman, Bella! I haven't betrayed my principles.

BELLA *[irritated]*. Wittering again! All that I said was that Rick *[Syrupy]* – with whom I have reached a very *personal* understanding – that Rick will be our new lipstick man for 'Merciless'. Taking over from Jean-Pierre. I'm sure that he can kiss just as well as our French dreamboy. Perhaps even better. Although I haven't had the opportunity to find out *[Much* *fluttering of eyelashes etc.]* – yet.

MELANIE. Sickening!

SYLVIA *[mischievously]*. Can he really kiss like Jean-Pierre? I hope Charlene won't be disappointed!

BELLA. Then we'll have to test him after all. Rick – take Patricia. Just a trial run, though. I don't want you developing a taste for her.

RICK *[very surprised]*. But you promised ...

BELLA. Did I? I can't remember promising anything. *[Harshly]* Just get on with it. Kiss her!

RICK. But you gave me your word ...

BELLA. And if I did? Who cares? *[To* 'PATRICIA'*]* Go on – kiss him!

'PATRICIA' *[helpless]*. But I can't do it.

BELLA. Kiss him! If you want to keep your job, that is.

MELANIE. This is awful, perverted. Why are you doing this?

CANDIDA *[spitefully]*. Because she's got the hots for 'Mr. Sex', that's why!

MELANIE. Bella, we are a *feminist* company.

BELLA. Yes, and I'm running it, remember? There's a good reason why your grandmother didn't put *you* in charge! The old biddy's not stupid. You couldn't run *a bath* properly, let alone a business enterprise! Now, stop meddling!

MELANIE. But you can't do this to poor Patricia …

BELLA. Oh, shut up! You're just a frustrated old lesbian. Patricia's not interested in you! And she's going to get the kiss of the century from Mr. Merciless, *right now*! *[To* RICK*]* Do it, Rick – take her! And make it big!

RICK. No, I can't.

PATRICK *[in his normal voice]*. And I can't either. *[Astonishment, gasps, expressions of surprise]*

SYLVIA. Patrick *[*ALL: *'Patrick? Patrick!']*, you had better tell them – or *show* them.

PATRICK *[revealing his identity]*. I'm not Patricia – I'm Patrick! *[To* MELANIE*]* Sorry, Melanie!

MELANIE. Oh, this is terrible! Monstrous! *[To* JULIA*]* Julia, I've been humiliated. Bella is sex-mad, and Patricia is a man. This is not a feminist company any more, it's rotten to the core. I don't know what to do!

JULIA. But I told you what to do. If you're the way you are, then *be* the way you are.

MELANIE. But I don't *know* if I'm ... you know ...

JULIA. Well, I know what *I* am ...

CANDIDA. Julia! Don't say that you're a ...

JULIA. And I know that I've got some work to do! *[She moves to exit]*

BELLA *[enraged]*. You stay here! Or you're fired! *[*JULIA *stops. Then, to everyone]* You're *all* fired! I'll run this company on my own!

BILL. Constructive downsizing! Dynamic management at its best!

BELLA *[to* BILL*]*. Oh, just shut up, Bullock! *[To* PATRICK*]* You have a lot to answer for, young man! You must think you're *very* clever.

PATRICK *[unrepentant]*. No, but I've made my point, haven't I? All that stuff about 'men' and 'women' – you're so full of hate, you couldn't even tell the difference. But I can do this job, and whether I'm Patrick or Patricia doesn't matter.

BELLA *[nastily]*. Isn't he cute, our little ambassador of the sexes? But I have one reason to thank you – you've given me a good excuse to clear up the rubbish in this organisation. And now we're going to see blood on the carpet!

SYLVIA *[to* MELANIE*]*. Melanie, if you want to save this company, you'd better do it now!

CANDIDA. I hate to say it, Melanie, but Sylvia's right. Only *you* can do it.

MELANIE *[helpless]*. But what?

JULIA. That's not so difficult, is it? Do it straight from the heart.

DESMOND *[taking centre stage]*. That is very good advice. There's so much pretending around here, paying lip service to love and emancipation and sexual equality, but it's really about power and money. And what are you selling? Lipstick, of all things! *[To* MELANIE*]* Be honest, young lady, and do what you think is best.

MELANIE *[taking a deep breath – then, to* BELLA*]*. Bella – you're fired. *[Stunned silence]* Pack your things, and leave this company. I'll talk to my grandmother. You'll get it in writing tomorrow.

BELLA *[contemptuously]*. And I thought I'd heard it all! Pathetic! And who's going to run Cosfem? Not *you*, surely?

MELANIE. No, you're right, I can't. *[Disheartened and*

unsure] There must be someone, though ...

CANDIDA *[seeing her opportunity]. I* could do it. No problem.

MELANIE *[relieved].* Yes! Candida would make a good chief executive. She knows about cosmetics ... and women ... – and men! And Sylvia and Julia and I will help, all in our different ways. We'll run Cosfem together!

BELLA *[raging].* This is illegal and ridiculous and inefficient and unfair and I won't stand for it and ...

MELANIE *[aware of the momentous nature of what she is saying].* Bella ... *[Pause]* Shut up! *[Tremendous applause from everyone except* BELLA *and* BILL*]* I'm serious, you've outstayed your welcome. Just call it quits, O.K.? And *your* services aren't required either, *Mr. Bullock*!

BILL *[with a touch of desparation].* But aren't you interested in my new concept?

MELANIE. No.

CANDIDA. No.

JULIA. Nope.

SYLVIA. No.

BELLA. Fine. Suit yourself. Without me, you can kiss all this good-bye sooner than you think.

SYLVIA. Maybe, but *you* can kiss it good-bye *right now*.

BELLA *[half-heartedly]*. Come along, Bullock, I've got a business proposal for you.

BILL. That's the spirit! Think positive, baby. Think constructive. Think *big*. There are big things we can do together. 'Bill and Bella's Active Marketing' – BABAM!! That has a ring to it! *[On their way out]* You and I will make a great team. There are new worlds to conquer! Let's get our heads together over a drink. I know a fantastic little place, just round the corner from here ... *[Exeunt* BELLA *and* BILL*]*

[20]

CANDIDA *[making herself comfortable in the Chief Executive's chair]*. I think I could get used to this chair. But there is a condition, darlings. I don't like this token man business. We need a few guys around the place, too, if only for decoration. We girls are still in charge, though. Now that's *my* idea of feminism! Can you live with that, Melanie?

MELANIE. I suppose so. As long as they are all as nice as Patrick ...

CANDIDA. And I expect to be addressed as Empress Candida from now on!

SYLVIA *[laughing]*. Cut it out, Candida!

CANDIDA. All right, all right! *[To everyone]* Good heavens, darlings, it *has* been an eventful day, if you'll pardon my language! And we've still got to film that ad! Get cracking, tomorrow is the big day! If we don't convince the shareholders, it's all been for nothing! And somebody call that Casket woman and tell her she isn't fired any longer.

Enter JOANNA *carrying yet more lips.*

JOANNA. Hello everyone. Lips on or lips off?

CANDIDA *[to* JOANNA, *with a gesture towards* RICK *and* CHARLENE*]*. Drop the lips, and get *those two* kissing!

JOANNA. Right, come on, we'll turn you into a pair of lovers such as the world has never seen.

RICK. Hey, you can't force these things! Charlene and I may have other plans, too. Nothing dramatic. I've been a sex idol for too long – now it's time to start being human again. That right, Charlene?

CHARLENE *[grasping for him]*. Yes, that's right, Rick. My, you *are* a hunk!

Exeunt CHARLENE, RICK, MELANIE *and* JOANNA.

JULIA. Let's get these lips to the P.R. department. You think you muscle-bound blokes could give me a hand? *[*JULIA, PATRICK *and* DESMOND *start picking up the lips]*

PATRICK *[jokingly]*. Hard labour wasn't mentioned in the contract!

SYLVIA. Would that be the contract that somebody called 'Patricia' signed?

PATRICK. Oh, damn.

DESMOND. You know, all this will make a great novel. Or maybe a play. I wonder what I should call it? *[*DESMOND *is lost in thought, looking at the huge lips in his hands]*

Exeunt PATRICK, JULIA and DESMOND.

SYLVIA. You're a natural for this, it seems.

CANDIDA. Thanks. But are you sure the commercial will work out? It wouldn't look good in my CV if I ran a company for a day and it got shut down.

SYLVIA. Don't worry about it, I've got a very good feeling about this one. Why don't we go and see what they're doing down there?

CANDIDA. Okay. *[They start moving offstage]* You know, you could always find a job in the burger-flipping sector?

SYLVIA. Sure. And you'd be a great cleaning-lady.

CANDIDA. Sylvia, I think this might be the beginning of a beautiful friendship ... *[Exeunt]*

Fade to black.

[video]

Scene with CHARLENE *and* RICK. *Their intense interest in each other is apparent in the way that they perform the scene.*

CHARLENE *[tenderly]*.
        I am a woman.

RICK *[simply]*.
        I am a man.

CHARLENE.
   In the life of a woman ... there are events.
There are events in which a woman is most a woman.
  There are events in which a woman is most herself.

RICK.
   In the life of a woman ... there is a man.

CHARLENE.
>For the man who matters
>And because I am a woman
>For those events ... and for that man
>There is ... *[Brandishing the lipstick]*
>Event.

They sink into a passionate kiss, falling down behind the props.

JOANNA *[off-camera].* And ... cut! That was just perfect, guys! If that doesn't convince them, nothing will. *[Pause]* Hey, it's okay now, we're finished. *[Pause]* I said we're finished ... Er, hello ... *[Hand-held camera follows behind scenery, unclearly recognises fumbling bodies, close-up of surprised red faces of* CHARLENE *and* RICK. *Freeze frame. Fade to black]*

End of the play

www.ingramcontent.com/pod-product-compliance
Lightning Source LLC
LaVergne TN
LVHW041632070426
835507LV00008B/569